how to get
planning
permission

By Roy Speer and Michael Dade

The rights of Roy Speer and Michael Dade to be identified
as authors of this Work have been asserted by them in
accordance with sections 77 and 78 of the Copyright,
Designs and Patents Act 1988.

First edition published 1995 by J M Dent Limited
Second edition published 1998 by Stonepound Books
Third edition published 2003 by Stonepound Books

FOURTH EDITION PUBLISHED BY OVOLO BOOKS

Text © Roy Speer and Michael Dade 1995-2010
This edition © Ovolo Books Ltd 2010
Printed in Great Britain by the MPG Books Group,
Bodmin and King's Lynn

ISBN 978 1 9059591 2 9

ACKNOWLEDGEMENTS
Thanks to the following for their help with the book:
the late Michael Cheal for his drawings and illustrations;
Constructive Individuals (www.constructiveindividuals.com)
and Woolhampton Design Centre (0118 9713363) for their
drawings; and Barry Page (www.barrypage.co.uk) for his
photos (Figure 16.6 and authors).

For more information please visit
www.ovolobooks.co.uk
or call 01480 891777 or email: info@ovolobooks.co.uk

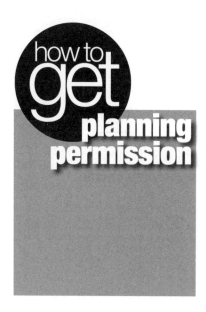

how to get planning permission

TESTIMONIALS

This book provides a no-nonsense guide to obtaining and renewing planning permission. With clear explanations, step-by-step instructions and sample documents it delivers exactly what the title says.

Jason Orme, Editor
Homebuilding & Renovating magazine

Modern planning is an extremely complex area, and anyone who is serious about building their own home should invest in this book to maximise the chance of building what they want, not to mention being forewarned about any nasty surprises. An essential read for all prospective builders.

Duncan Hayes, Editor
Build It magazine

Obtaining planning permission is an essential part of the design process, especially if architects want to earn their fee. As architects we often pretend to know the answers, but do we? This book is an essential source of reference to the architect in private practice.

George Baxter, ARIBA
Chartered Architect, writer and lecturer

This book is the distillation of years of experience in gaining planning consent for clients. It describes simply and accurately when you need planning permission and how to obtain it. A must have for selfbuilders and extenders.

Ross Stokes
Editor, Selfbuild & Design magazine.

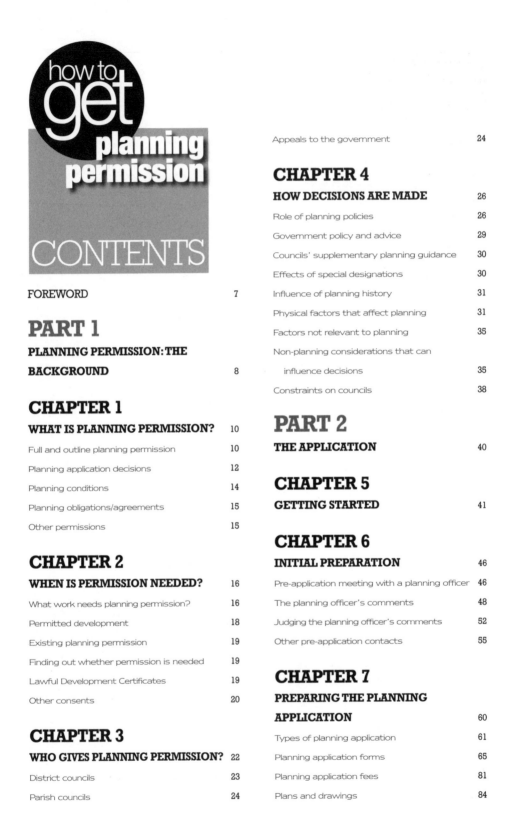

how to get planning permission

CONTENTS

CHAPTER 8
THE PLANNING APPLICATION 100

CHAPTER 9
DEVELOPMENT WITHOUT
PERMISSION 122

PART 3
MAKING A PLANNING APPEAL 126

CHAPTER 10
FIRST CONSIDERATIONS 127

CHAPTER 11
PREPARING FOR AN APPEAL 134

CHAPTER 12
CONDUCTING THE APPEAL 144

PART 4
PERMISSION FOR NEW HOMES 154

CHAPTER 13
SITE CONSIDERATIONS 155

how to get planning permission updates

GETPLANNINGPERMISSION.CO.UK

FOREWORD

We hope you find this book as helpful as have the many people who've contacted us since the publication of the first edition of 'How to Get Planning Permission' in 1995. The planning system, procedures and requirements have changed very significantly in these last 15 years and, sad to say, these changes haven't been to the advantage of applicants.

Government attempts to simplify and streamline the system have, hitherto, only served to make it progressively more complicated, obscure and expensive for users. And yet despite this, there are still many things you can do – armed with inside knowledge – to maximise your chances of getting planning permission.

In this book, we aim to cut through the jargon and myriad technicalities to give you step-by-step guidance on how to get the most from the system. Government revision of planning shows no sign of abating and further change is on the way.

The book is based on current law and regulations for England. Although the planning system is similar throughout the UK, there are differences in detail and terminology between the countries and we draw attention to some of these in the text.

For the foregoing reasons, it's vital to double check crucial details – such as time limits and precise procedural requirements – before taking action. A book isn't a substitute for specific advice on your particular circumstances. Many of the readers who contact us do so to find out whether we might be able to help them professionally through our consultancy practice and we have indeed been able to take on some of those cases, helping readers from all over the country. Our office numbers and email addresses are at the end of the book.

We thank the people who kindly supplied example drawings and photos reproduced in the book. Their names and contacts are in the acknowledgements.

Finally, we wish you success with all your planning proposals and hope that you find this book a suitable introduction to a system that manages to be contrary, bureaucratic and frustrating in equal measure!

PART 1
PLANNING PERMISSION: THE BACKGROUND

You want to build your own house, or to extend it, or to carry out alterations. You know what you want to build. You can find out how much it will cost and decide who'll do the work. But then there's planning permission. What is planning permission? Do you need it? Who gives it? How's the decision made? The answers to these questions aren't always easy to find out.

Planning permission can be a complex subject. The people you might turn to immediately – builders, solicitors or architects – often don't fully understand all the technicalities, procedural requirements and tactical points. In the first part of this book, we look at the basics of planning permission – what it is, when you need it, who grants it, and how it's decided.

PLANNING APPLICATION ACTION CHECKLIST

1 decide what you want to do

2 decide what help you need, such as planning consultant and building designer

3 prepare or commission a sketch scheme

4 discuss your proposal with a planning officer

5 find out what application documents are required

6 review your proposal in light of the planning officer's comments

7 carry out any other pre-application consultations

8 commission application drawings and any statements/reports required

9 obtain and complete planning application forms

10 write or commission a supporting letter/planning statement

11 check the planning application fee

12 submit the application to the council

13 check the council's acknowledgement letter or contact the council if the letter doesn't arrive within a week

14 read letters and consultee responses

15 check progress of the application with the planning officer

16 submit further information and/or revise the application, if necessary

17 read the planning officer's report (committee decision)

18 contact councillor (committee decision)

19 attend committee meeting and speak, if appropriate

20 study decision notice

21 if approved, apply for approval of reserved matters or to discharge conditions

22 if refused, consider re-applying and/or appealing the decision

You will need planning permission to build your dream home – and it's not automatic

Most extensions also require permission and there are strict rules about what you can do

background
1

CHAPTER 1

WHAT IS PLANNING PERMISSION?

Planning permission is the authority required by law to carry out development. New building work is development, as are changes of use, such as converting buildings into houses or using houses for non-residential purposes.

Planning permission is sometimes referred to as 'planning consent' and 'planning approval', but all these terms have exactly the same meaning. Anyone who wants planning permission to carry out building work must make a planning application, which involves completing forms and showing the proposed building on drawings. Most planning applications are decided by local councils.

FULL AND OUTLINE PLANNING PERMISSION

There are two types of planning permission – planning permission and outline planning permission (planning permission in principle in Scotland). The former is usually called 'full planning permission' or 'detailed planning permission' to distinguish it from outline. In applications for full planning permission, you must give all the details of your proposed building. Application drawings need to show where the building will be sited, the access drive, parking spaces, floor and roof plans, what each elevation, or side, of the building will look like, and any alterations to existing buildings. An example is shown in Figure 1.1 below.

Outline planning applications, on the other hand, are made when you want to establish, in principle, whether a new building will be permitted. You have only to provide maximum dimensions, number of units and an indication of the layout and access but can leave out some or all of the details and apply for approval of them later. You can't make outline applications for changes of use and so can't apply in outline for conversions. Nor can you make outline applications in Conservation Areas and in other sensitive locations the council can insist on the submission of more detail.

Figure 1.1

Fully detailed drawings are required to accompany a full planning application

Outline applications are usually made:

■ when you're uncertain about the prospects of getting planning permission;

■ to avoid the expense of having full drawings prepared at an early stage;

■ where design might be controversial;

■ where you don't intend to carry out the work but want to sell the site with planning permission.

After outline planning permission is granted, the details – layout, scale, appearance, access and landscaping – can be put forward in another type of application, called a 'reserved matters' application. When both outline planning permission and the reserved matters have been approved by the council, the two together are the equivalent of a full permission. Reserved matters applications have to be made within three years of the outline planning permission. You can make any number of different reserved matters applications on the same outline planning permission but only one can be carried out. This is why outline planning applications are useful where design is going to be controversial, as a number of

different detailed schemes can be put forward for approval.

PLANNING APPLICATION DECISIONS

The result of a planning application is given in a decision notice, sent to the applicant or the applicant's agent. A decision notice is a formal-looking document using plenty of planning jargon that's not always easy to understand. The decision notice sets out what the application was for, who made the application, the address of the site and whether permission is granted or refused.

Although the name of the person who made the application is recorded both on the application forms and in the decision notice, planning permission applies to the site in question, not to the person who got the permission.

When permission is granted the council can make the planning permission subject to various conditions. These conditions are listed in the decision notice together with the council's justification for them (see Figure 1.2 opposite). The decision notice also contains a short statement of the council's reason for giving permission.

DECISION NOTICE GRANTING PLANNING PERMISSION

STOPPLE DISTRICT COUNCIL

Mr I & Mrs P Bestead
92 Monarch Avenue
West Simple
VC8 0DX   09/01643/COU

TOWN AND COUNTRY PLANNING ACT 1990

PERMISSION
Description: Change of use from nursing home to single dwelling.
                     Removal of fire escape staircase and alterations.

Location: 75 Cindergrind Road Stickey Common VC10 2PS
The Council hereby notify you that they GRANT planning permission for
the above development to be carried out in accordance with the submitted
application and plans and subject to compliance with the following
conditions:-
1.   The development hereby permitted shall be begun before the
         expiration of 3 years from the date of this permission.

Reason: To comply with Section 91 of the Town and Country Planning Act 1990.

2.   The windows on the south western (side) elevation of the
         building shall at all times be glazed with obscured glass.

Reason: To protect the amenities and privacy of the adjoining property and
        to accord with Policy D3 of the Stopple District Local Plan and
        Policy DOS1 of the adopted North Bustle Structure Plan 2001–2016.

INFORMATIVES
1.   You are advised that the District Council determined this
         application on the basis of the following drawings:
         208/035/JE01 date stamped 27 October 2009
         208/035/JE02 date stamped 27 October 2009

Reason for Decision
1.   The proposal accords with Policy D3 of the Stopple District Local
         Plan in that the new use does not lead to an unacceptable increase
         in activity such as to harm the character and amenity of the
         locality or the amenities of neighbouring residents.
         This Information is only intended as a summary of the reasons for
         grant of planning permission. For further detail on the decision
         please come and view the planning file at the council offices during
         normal working hours.

Norbert Butster

DISTRICT PLANNER   10 DEC 2009
NB: IT IS IMPORTANT THAT YOU SHOULD READ THE NOTES ACCOMPANYING THIS FORM

Figure 1.2

When planning permission is refused, the notice sets out the reasons for the council's refusal. These reasons are rarely written in plain English, so unless you're familiar with the convoluted language used by councils, you might be at a loss to know what they actually mean (see Figure 8.4 on page 115).

PLANNING CONDITIONS

One condition which planning permission always specifies is the time within which the work must be started. In most cases, the period is three years. Unless the work is begun within the stated time limit, or the permission is renewed, planning permission simply expires and a new planning application is then needed. Some conditions are standard, for example the requirement for external building materials to be approved by the council or, in the case of outline planning permission, the requirement for the design and layout to be approved. Beyond these, conditions can cover a wide range of factors relating to the design and use of buildings and can also apply to adjoining land which an applicant owns or occupies. For example, conditions on planning permissions can:

■ require existing buildings to be demolished before new ones are built;
■ stop some future alterations (eg dormer windows);
■ ensure certain windows have obscured glass;
■ control the sequence of building (eg constructing access roads before buildings are built);
■ specify the location of the access;
■ ensure car parking spaces are provided;
■ make small modifications to a proposed building (eg use of materials);
■ in exceptional circumstances, restrict who can occupy a building (eg agricultural workers' houses);
■ make permission temporary (eg mobile home).

There are, however, limits to the scope of conditions on a planning permission: they must be necessary, relevant, capable of being enforced by the council, precise and reasonable. These are examples of conditions which shouldn't be put on planning permissions:

■ delay carrying out building work;
■ require part of the site to be

given for the construction of a public road or footpath;

■ limit the number of people who can occupy a building;

■ oblige an applicant to pay money to the council.

PLANNING OBLIGATIONS/ AGREEMENTS

There's another way of controlling new building, which has wider scope than planning conditions. This is the use of legal undertakings made by applicants. The formal title of these is 'planning obligations', but they're sometimes known as 'planning agreements' or alternatively 'section 106 agreements' ('article 40' in Northern Ireland or 'section 75' in Scotland) because they're usually negotiated and agreed between councils and applicants. Planning obligations can be put forward by applicants without the council's agreement. Planning obligations are legally binding documents which oblige applicants to carry out works, make financial payments towards infrastructure improvements, or regulate the building in some way. Whilst conditions are attached to every planning permission, planning obligations are signed in far

fewer single house or small scale residential schemes.

OTHER PERMISSIONS

There are other consents, apart from planning permission, that might be needed before work is carried out. Any work affecting a Listed Building must have separate Listed Building Consent and demolition in a Conservation Area requires Conservation Area Consent. These consents are similar to planning permission and applications for them are usually made at the same time as planning applications. Most new building work needs building regulations approval, which deals with health, safety and structural soundness of buildings. Although sometimes dealt with by councils' planning departments, building regulations are a technical subject and come under a completely different set of rules to planning.

background

1

CHAPTER 2

WHEN IS PLANNING PERMISSION NEEDED?

The answer to this question isn't always straightforward and there are various rules and exceptions which can complicate the issue. Finding out about the need for planning permission is important – carrying out unauthorised work isn't in itself a criminal offence, but councils have powers to stop work that doesn't have permission and costly mistakes can be made.

The first step towards finding out whether you need planning permission is to decide precisely what it is you want to do. There are some grey areas in planning rules and unless you know exactly what your project involves, it could be difficult to establish beyond doubt the need for planning permission.

WHAT WORK NEEDS PLANNING PERMISSION?

Planning permission is needed for 'development', which means new buildings, building work, and changes in the use of property. New buildings are the

PLANNING PERMISSION NEEDED	PLANNING PERMISSION NOT NEEDED
building and re-building	maintenance and repair
demolition of houses	minor alterations and improvement not affecting external appearance
extensions and conservatories	internal work and alterations
basements	re-roofing
dormer windows	exterior painting
chimneys	forming window and door openings not affecting appearance
satellite dishes	like-for-like replacement windows
fire escapes	TV aerials
forming accesses	taking in lodger or small-scale bed and breakfast use
laying hardstandings	converting or using outbuildings in garden in connection with house
swimming pools	stationing a caravan or mobile home in garden used with the house
garages and outbuildings	small-scale business use in part of house or in outbuilding
incorporating agricultural land into gardens	
sub-dividing property into separate dwellings	
using single dwelling as house in multiple occupation	
living in self-contained outbuilding or mobile home separate from house	
living in caravan on house-building site while not being involved in the project full time	
living in a mobile or park home on agricultural land	

Notes: permitted development rights give automatic permission in some circumstances (see Parts Four and Five)
planning conditions and legal agreements can restrict what you can otherwise do without applying for planning permission

Figure 2.1

obvious structures like houses, garages and outbuildings and rebuilding must also have planning permission, even if you replace exactly what was there before.

Building work covers other types of construction – walls, fences, drives, swimming pools – and can include alterations to existing buildings – extensions, new roof structures, making new window openings, demolition and partial demolition. Internal alterations don't need planning permission (although they might need building regulations approval). Maintenance, improvement and minor external alterations to buildings are also outside the official definition of 'development', and so planning permission isn't required.

Changes in the use of property means changing between different categories of use, for example houses to shops, or houses to hotels, and the same applies to land – buying part of a farmer's field and including it in your garden is a change of use from agriculture to residential amenity land. Partial changes of use don't always have to have permission – the most common example is running a business from home where, as long as the over all use remains domestic, planning permission isn't necessary. Using any building in the grounds of a house for any normal domestic purposes connected with the house also doesn't need planning permission. Some projects, for example, barn conversions, involve both building work and a change of use but

one planning application covers both aspects. See the panel on the previous page for examples of projects that do and don't need planning permission.

PERMITTED DEVELOPMENT
The legal definition of what work must have planning permission is wide-reaching and some of this work is of very little consequence. The planning system would grind to a halt if a planning application had to be made for every single minor project, so to get around this, there are rules that allow some types of development to go ahead without a planning application. This is called 'permitted development'.

Under the permitted development rules, planning permission is granted automatically for different kinds of work, such as extensions, outbuildings, fences and hard standings. In each case there are specified limits and exceptions and the interpretation of the rules isn't always straightforward. We'll be looking at permitted development rights relevant to various kinds of project in Part Five. In limited situations, councils can take away any automatic permitted development rights and this is most commonly done in Conservation Areas. The council makes what's called an 'article 4 direction', which is a legal document showing the area affected and the rights that are taken away.

EXISTING PLANNING PERMISSION

We've seen that planning permission relates to the property and not to the owner or person who made the planning application. Where planning permission has already been granted, you can take advantage of it. Look carefully at existing permissions, checking that the planning permission:

■ hasn't expired;

■ is for exactly what you want to do;

■ doesn't contain unacceptable conditions;

■ is either a full permission or, if in outline, whether details have been approved or would be approved for what you want.

FINDING OUT WHETHER PERMISSION IS NEEDED

Probably the simplest and quickest way to find out if you need planning permission is to ask the council. Speak to a planning officer

about your proposal – he or she should be able to tell you whether to make a planning application, or what other information he needs in order to decide. You must judge the planning officer's comments carefully as there are reasons – which we come to later – why they might err on the side of caution. If you're told a planning application isn't required, try to get this confirmed in writing.

As an alternative to speaking to the council, or if you have doubts about what the planning officer said, you can take professional advice from a planning consultant. Be wary about relying just on what a builder or contractor tells you, as they might be more interested in getting on with the job than the technicalities of planning law. Remember, it's likely to be you who would suffer the consequences of a mistake over the need for planning permission.

LAWFUL DEVELOPMENT CERTIFICATES

There's a formal way to find out if planning permission is needed – by making a special type of application to the district council for a Lawful Development Certificate. You can apply either before or after work takes place, although it's much safer to apply beforehand. There are certain circumstances where you would apply after the work has taken place, such as when a previous owner has carried out work without planning permission and you want to establish that permission wasn't in fact needed.

If there's doubt over whether planning permission is required, it's usually best to make a planning application anyway. Think about applying for a Lawful Development Certificate instead if the council is likely to refuse planning permission or to attach unwelcome conditions to a permission. With Lawful Development Certificates, the council is supposed to give a purely legal answer – planning permission is needed or isn't needed. Whether the council likes the details of the particular proposal shouldn't come into it.

OTHER CONSENTS

We've noted that there are other types of permission you might

Figure 2.2

Most new construction, like this addition of a first floor, requires planning permission

need. Carrying out work on a
Listed Building and demolishing
a building in a Conservation
Area without the necessary
permissions are criminal offences
and large fines can be given. Don't
take chances in these situations
and check with the council. If it
says permission isn't needed, get
written confirmation.

background

1

CHAPTER 3

WHO GIVES PLANNING PERMISSION?

The planning system is run by both central and local government. For administrative purposes, England and Northern Ireland are divided into counties and each county is divided into district, borough or city authorities. A small number of English authorities are single-tier councils, having all local government responsibilities, rather than these being split between a county and district council. These are called unitary authorities and they include all councils in English metropolitan areas. Scotland and Wales are divided entirely into single-tier council areas. In Wales these are called county or county borough councils. For convenience, we shall refer to all councils, apart from English county councils, as 'district councils'.

Planning applications for new houses and work related to houses are made to the district council for the area. In Northern Ireland, planning applications are decided by a branch of central government – the Planning

Service of the Department of the Environment – which has six divisional offices around the province. In National Parks, the respective National Park Authority deals with all planning matters.

DISTRICT COUNCILS

The name and address of your district council, or the district council which covers the area where the property is located, can be found in Yellow Pages or on Yell.com under 'Local Government'. District councils are made up of elected councillors and employees of the council, called officers. Most district councils have about 45–55 councillors who are locally elected politicians representing national or local political parties or are independent. Councillors are laymen and not qualified in planning and whilst some develop a good grasp of the subject, others don't.

The various responsibilities are dealt with by different departments, one of which is the planning department. Some district councils amalgamate planning with other departments and give them grand names such as 'Environmental and Technical Services', but they're still the planning department. The number of employees in a planning department varies depending on the size and nature of the area covered. Both planning officers and support staff work in these departments. Most planning officers have professional town planning qualifications; few have experience outside the world of local government.

The job of the planning department is to receive and process planning applications. The officers assess applications, carry out consultation and write a report on the proposal, ending with their recommendation on whether they think planning permission should be given. Minor and unopposed planning applications are decided by planning officers – these are called 'delegated decisions' as the authority to make the decision is delegated to planning officers by the councillors.

Large-scale or contentious proposals are decided by councillors and out of the total number of councillors about 10 to 20 will be on the planning applications committee. Regular committee meetings are held, at which councillors work through the planning officers' reports and make decisions on applications.

In Northern Ireland, applications are assessed by development control officers and decided by the Divisional Planning Manager. District councillors are consulted and there's a procedure for resolving cases where they don't agree with the officers.

PARISH COUNCILS

Within some council areas there are parish, community and town councils and in this book we refer to all of these as 'parish councils'. There's a great deal of confusion over the role of parish councils in deciding planning applications. Parish councils are consulted about applications but have no power to make decisions about them. Although parish councillors might have influence over planning decisions, this is something quite different and will be referred to in Chapter 4.

APPEALS TO THE GOVERNMENT

If planning permission is refused by the district council, the person who made the application can appeal against the council's decision. Similarly, if planning permission is given but with conditions, the applicant can appeal against

any or all of those conditions. Appeals are made to: The Planning Inspectorate in England and Wales; the Directorate for Planning and Environmental Appeals in Scotland; and the Planning Appeals Commission in Northern Ireland.

The Planning Inspectorate is an executive agency of the Department of Communities and Local Government (DCLG) and Welsh Assembly, based in Bristol, which appoints planning inspectors to consider and decide appeals. In Scotland appeals are dealt with by reporters appointed by the Directorate for Planning and Environmental Appeals of the Scottish Executive based in Edinburgh and in Northern Ireland the Planning Appeals Commission appoints commissioners to decide appeals. Inspectors, reporters and commissioners are experienced professionals – surveyors, town planners, engineers, solicitors – who work full or part time for their respective agencies. For convenience, we'll generally refer to all of these as 'inspectors'.

The decision on an appeal is given in a letter sent to the person who made the appeal, and to the district council, setting out the reasons for making the decision

OPERATING THE PLANNING SYSTEM

National oversight	Personnel	Functions
Secretary of State DCLG (England)	Members of the	Draw up national
Scottish Executive (Scotland)	government	policy
National Assembly for Wales (Wales)	Civil servants	Oversee the
Northern Ireland Assembly (Northern Ireland)		planning system
		Decide major planning
		appeals
National Planning	**Personnel**	**Functions**
Planning Inspectorate (England	Planning inspectors	Scrutinise council draft
& Wales)		planning policy
Directorate for Planning and	Reporters	documents
Environmental Appeals (Scotland)		Decide planning
Planning Appeals Commission (Northern	Commissioners	appeals
Ireland)		
Local Planning	**Personnel**	**Functions**
District, borough and city councils (England)	Elected councillors	Draw up planning
Councils (Scotland)	Planning officers	policy documents
County and county borough Councils (Wales)		Decide planning
Divisional offices, Department		applications
of the Environment (Northern Ireland)		Take enforcement
		action

Figure 3.1

The planning system is administered by various levels of government and you might need to deal with all of them

(see Figure 12.1 on pages 148–149). Decision letters are, in effect, like councils' decision notices as they also grant or refuse planning permission and conditions can be attached.

background

1

CHAPTER 4

HOW DECISIONS ARE MADE

We know what planning permission is, when it's needed and who gives it, so let's look at the most important question of all – what determines whether planning permission's given or refused? The law lays down the basis for deciding planning applications: councils, and inspectors on appeal, have to follow approved planning policies, as set out in development plans, unless 'material considerations' indicate otherwise. We'll look first at planning policies and then at all the other factors that can be material to decision making.

ROLE OF PLANNING POLICIES

The system of planning policy documents is changing. Planning policies used to be set out in Structure Plans and Local Plans. Welsh councils and English unitary authorities produced Unitary Development Plans (UDPs), which were like Structure and Local Plans but contained in one document. For convenience

Figure 4.1

Councils' planning policy documents are the starting point for deciding whether permission will be given

we'll use the term 'Local Plan' to include Unitary Development Plans. Structure Plans covered counties or a number of council areas and set out a broad strategy for development. Local Plans were drawn up by district councils within the framework provided by the Structure Plan, translating the broad development strategy to the district, and applying the general Structure Plan policies for all types of development, to the specific area (see Figure 4.1 above).

The new system is far more complicated and ridden with bewildering jargon and initials. Planning policies are now to be set out in Local Development Frameworks (LDFs) in England, Local Development Plans (LDPs) in Scotland and Wales, and in Development Plans in Northern Ireland. We'll use the initials LDF to cover all these plans. In Scotland, groups of councils, called strategic development planning authorities (SDPAs), will draw up Strategic Development Plans (SDPs) which will replace Structure Plans.

Planning policy documents consist of a written part, setting out the district council's development policies, and a proposals map. Local Plans contained all the policies in one document; LDFs comprise a number of documents. The written parts of these documents distinguish the actual planning policies from the accompanying explanation and justification. A proposals map shows the area covered by the document, indicating where various policies apply and identifying individual sites for development. Selected areas are shown in greater detail on inset maps, where this is necessary to make the policies clear.

Planning policies can:

■ be general and apply throughout the area (eg standards for building design);

■ relate to specific areas (eg Conservation Areas);

■ categorise settlements (eg specify the towns and villages where new houses will and won't be allowed);

■ concern certain types of development (eg house extensions);

■ show how a particular site should be developed (eg site allocated for new houses).

One of the main functions of most planning policy documents is to distinguish between towns/villages and the countryside. This is done to contain most new development within urban areas, to control the expansion of built-up areas, and to limit new building in the countryside. The boundaries defining urban areas are given names such as 'Settlement Boundary', 'Built-up Area', 'Village Envelope' and 'Housing Framework'. A second important function in many Local Plan/LDFs is to set out what type of development will be permitted in various categories of town/village, such as large-scale house building, small infill schemes or affordable housing only. Policy documents have guidelines for the main kinds of development and policies relevant to residential development are likely to be in sections dealing with:

■ housing – amount and location of new housing, housing types, replacements and conversions;

■ built environment – design, effect on neighbours, extensions and alterations, landscaping;

■ conservation – building

design and materials, building in Conservation Areas, work on Listed Buildings;

■ countryside – restraint on building outside urban areas, building in Green Belts, Areas of Outstanding Natural Beauty/ National Scenic Areas, agricultural dwellings.

Examples of planning policies are given in Figures 14.2, 16.2 and 17.2. Two points are immediately clear from the examples: first, there's a jargon used in planning which doesn't help public understanding of the system it's supposed to serve; and second, planning policies can appear rather negative which is symptomatic of the way certain councils and planning officers seem to deal with planning. Not all areas are covered by an up-to-date policy document that's been through all the formal preparation stages, but many are. Where there's no recent approved policy document, or where a new one's being drawn up, the policies of a draft plan can be taken into account. The weight put on them depends on how far advanced the plan is in the preparation process. Watch out for new policy documents coming through the process as they can introduce

changes which could be significant. It might be advantageous to get your application submitted quickly or to wait until a new policy has come into effect.

It is then the policies of the old-style or new-style policy documents against which a planning application should primarily be judged. This might sound like a straightforward matter, but unfortunately it isn't. Policies can contradict each other, point in different directions or be open to different interpretations. Whilst planning policies are the starting point for decisions, there are other 'material considerations' which have to be taken into account.

GOVERNMENT POLICY AND ADVICE ON PLANNING

The government publishes its own national planning policies, which district councils are meant to follow, both in decision making and in drawing up Local Plan and now LDF policies. Government policies are set out in circulars and, in England, Planning Policy Guidance Notes (PPGs) and Statements (PPSs); in Scotland, Scottish Planning Policy (SPP), National Planning Policy Guidelines (NPPGs) and Planning Advice Notes (PANs); in Wales, Technical Advice Notes (TANs); and in Northern Ireland, Planning Policy Statements (PPSs) and Development Control Advice Notes (DCANs). These documents often give useful background and summaries of the law on the particular topic. Some is general, such as guidance on housing provision, but some is quite detailed, such as building in Conservation Areas and the proper use of conditions on planning permissions. The guidance is on the government websites, or district council planning departments have copies of the documents which you can see.

COUNCILS' SUPPLEMENTARY PLANNING GUIDANCE/ DOCUMENTS

In addition to Local Plans and LDFs, councils sometimes produce other statements and leaflets setting out their views and guidance. This informal policy can cover advice on design and layout, trees and development or car parking and access. These booklets can be helpful although they don't have the same status as officially approved policies. They're intended to provide guidance, which shouldn't be applied rigidly by councils (but often is).

EFFECTS OF SPECIAL DESIGNATIONS

In planning, there are special designations which can apply to individual buildings or wide areas of land. The most common are:
■ Conservation Areas – parts of towns or villages with special historic or architectural character;
■ Listed Buildings – individual buildings or structures with particular historic or architectural merit;
■ Tree Preservation Orders – protection given to individual trees, groups of trees or whole woodlands;
■ Areas of Outstanding Natural Beauty or National Scenic Areas in Scotland – areas of particularly attractive countryside.

There are rules on how each designation should be taken into account in deciding planning applications and additional controls on work affecting Listed Buildings and demolition in Conservation Areas. Where a specially designated building or area is concerned, the council must consider how it would be affected by a proposed development, in light of the designation.

INFLUENCE OF PLANNING HISTORY

In some cases there are previous planning applications or existing buildings and uses on the site to take into account, and this can influence decisions either way. Where there are previous permissions, there's normally little justification for refusing a similar application.

There might be an existing house, or some other occupied building on the site. Unless that building has particular historic or architectural value or is covered by a special designation, its replacement will generally be accepted. Where a site is used for an unpleasant use, like a scrap yard in a mainly residential area, granting planning permission can be a useful way of getting rid of it. On the other hand, where a site has a string of refused planning permissions going back years, another application of exactly the same type is unlikely to succeed.

The size of an existing building on a site can limit the size of a replacement or an extension

that's allowed. Previous planning applications could have gone to appeal, and appeal decisions are an especially important part of the planning history of a site as good reasons must exist to depart from what a planning inspector has said, unless circumstances have changed in the meantime.

Appeal decisions aren't always clear. They can be turned down on points of detail, but the principle of the proposal be endorsed. Interpretations are often disputed between applicants and councils.

PHYSICAL FACTORS THAT AFFECT PLANNING DECISIONS

The points covered so far, despite being crucial to the decision, might appear a little abstract. We now look at the more practical factors that also determine whether planning permission is granted. Some of these are illustrated in Figure 4.2 overleaf.

SIZE AND SHAPE OF SITE

The development needs to respect the intended site; off-the-peg designs don't always fit neatly in to awkwardly shaped pieces of land, and buildings must have adequate amenity space around them.

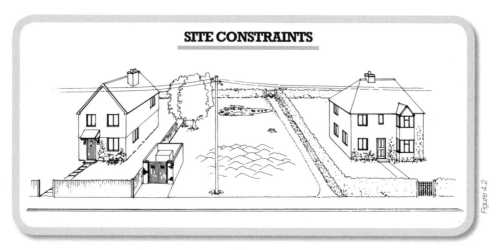

SITE CONSTRAINTS

Figure 4.2

Physical site constraints that influence whether you can get planning permission include: overlooking from neighbouring houses; trees; obstacles, such as sub-stations and telegraph poles; filled ground; drains, indicated by manhole covers; wet ground and footpaths

TOPOGRAPHY

The lie of the land influences whether buildings can be built at all and the form they take. Changes in level or undulations, used creatively, can help screen buildings but can also make buildings appear prominent.

GROUND CONDITIONS

The sort of conditions that affect planning permission decisions are: land liable to flood; contaminated land; unstable land; ground made up by tipping or filling; and areas affected by mining subsidence. Some of these can be overcome and special foundations, protection measures or cleaning up can be

proposed or included as conditions on a planning permission.

ARCHAEOLOGICAL REMAINS

The existence of known remains can influence development; the location, rarity, importance and extent of the find are relevant factors and excavation or avoidance might be required.

EFFECT ON EXISTING BUILDINGS

Buildings already on site are taken into account: extensions and alterations will affect appearance; new construction close to buildings might affect the setting; and buildings to be re-used must be physically suitable to accommodate proposed new uses.

BOUNDARIES

Hedges, trees, fences and walls can screen new buildings, or might enhance the area when provided as part of the scheme. On the other hand, the loss of important existing boundary features can sometimes have an undesirable effect and their removal can open up views and make new buildings too prominent.

SERVICES

New buildings need services – drainage, water, gas, electricity and telephone lines. Drainage is the most significant for planning purposes and councils must ensure the site can be drained before granting planning permission. The presence of services running through, over or near the site affects where development is allowed to take place, although some of these obstacles can be moved.

TREES

Trees and other vegetation often restrict development, but sometimes they do provide opportunities to create a high-quality setting and help new buildings blend into the environment. The following points are considered:

■ number of trees to be lost, their age, expected life span, and importance in views and for screening;
■ amount of pruning or cutting back needed;
■ effect of construction on roots;
■ the likelihood of further trees being removed;
■ distance between building and trees.

Trees that make a valuable contribution to the area can be protected by Tree Preservation Orders (TPOs). This gives the trees additional status in weighing up decisions on planning applications. As a result of this, councils sometimes use TPOs as a means to try to thwart development proposals they don't like.

WILDLIFE

The existence of rare or protected animals and plants on or near a site can affect the principle or siting of development.

ACCESS

Two issues arise here – highway safety and environmental considerations. Highway authorities set standards for accesses and of these visibility and on-site turning are most important.

Apart from on housing estates and lightly used roads, drivers leaving a site must be able to see an adequate distance in either direction to avoid the risk of collision, and drivers on the road must be able to see vehicles emerging. Cars should be able to drive forwards in and out of a site. Bends, narrow carriageways, hills and the existence of other nearby accesses can all affect highway safety.

Environmental factors include the appearance of the access itself, the effect of forming openings and visibility splays (see Figure 7.3 on page 69) at access points involving removal of important hedges and trees and disturbance caused by vehicles using the access.

CAR PARKING

Councils set guidelines for the number of spaces required for various types of dwelling, such as one space for a flat, two spaces for a three-bed house, three spaces for a four-bed house.

RIGHTS OF WAY

The existence of a public right of way doesn't necessarily stop planning permission being granted but it must be capable of being relocated along an equally convenient route, if it's in the way of a building. This is dealt with by a diversion order under different procedures.

NEIGHBOURS

One of the council's main concerns is the effect of development on neighbouring residents. Development shouldn't cause loss of privacy in private areas inside or outside adjoining properties or in the new building itself. This is determined by the relative position of windows, view points and gardens. 'Overlooking', as it's called in planning jargon, is subjective and not by any means an exact science. It doesn't mean rooms or gardens mustn't be seen from anywhere. New building shouldn't block out natural daylight or prevent occupants seeing out of windows, especially habitable rooms which include large kitchens, living rooms, dining rooms and bedrooms. Similarly, new development mustn't be overbearing or cause extensive overshadowing in gardens. Potential noise and disturbance is also taken into account. This is often a factor where an access drive passes close to an adjoining house but normal domestic activity is, of course, to be expected.

SURROUNDING AREA

Proposals ought to be compatible with the area in which they're located and must be sited and designed so as to be visually acceptable in their own right, and also to fit in with existing buildings around them. This doesn't mean they have to be exactly the same as other buildings – they can differ in style so long as that difference doesn't cause any harm. This is largely a matter of personal opinion and the points looked for in assessing compatibility include height, proportions, size, roof lines, building materials and window patterns. New buildings shouldn't clash with established patterns of development which are formed by:
■ the relationship between buildings;
■ the relationship between buildings, roads and footpaths;
■ plot sizes;
■ the position of buildings within plots;
■ sizes of buildings.

Where areas have a prevailing style or pattern of buildings that's obviously worth preserving, a Conservation Area might be designated by the district council. Development here is looked at closely to ensure it blends in with, or compliments, the area. Similarly, new building near a Listed Building mustn't harm its setting.

FACTORS NOT RELEVANT TO PLANNING

It's hard to say that any particular factor is never relevant to the decision on a planning application but all should relate in some way to the use of property or its physical development. There are some that generally shouldn't be taken into account. These are listed in Figure 4.3 (see over page).

NON-PLANNING CONSIDERATIONS THAT CAN INFLUENCE DECISIONS

So far in this chapter we've looked at all the factors that should be taken into account – approved planning policies and material considerations. That's how fair and rational decisions on planning applications are supposed to be made. The flaw in the theory is that the planning system is operated by human beings and,

FACTORS WHICH AFFECT
PLANNING DECISIONS

Government planning
guidance
Local development
framework/plan or
development plan policy
Local plan policy
Council supplementary
planning guidance
Special designations (Green
Belt, Conservation Area,
Area of Outstanding Natural
Beauty/National Scenic
Area)
Size and shape of site
Size, position and

prominence of buildings
Relationship with other
property
Pattern of development
Site layout and space around
buildings
Amount of garden
Trees and hedges
Access, parking and turning
space
Drainage
Overlooking and loss of
outlook
Noise and disturbance
Over-shadowing

Character of the area
Effect on setting
Design and appearance
Effect on landscape
Type of materials
Compatibility with existing
buildings
Flood risk
Access to facilities and public
transport
Energy use
Public rights of way
Effect on ecology and wildlife

FACTORS WHICH SHOULD NOT
AFFECT PLANNING DECISIONS

Structural stability (new
builds)
Stability of adjoining
buildings
Safety of materials
Methods of construction
Boundary and neighbour
disputes
Private rights of way
Legal rights of access
Covenants

Rights of light
Access to maintain other
property
Personal circumstances
Identity of applicant or
objectors
How long applicant lived in
area
Motives of applicant
Financial viability or profit
Loss of private views

Values of property
Supervision and standard of
work
Disruption during building
work
Benefits unrelated to
proposal
Number of objections
Relationships with
councillors or council
employees

Figure 4.3

A wide range of factors affect planning decisions but there are some which shouldn't normally be considered human nature being what it is, other considerations inevitably come into play from time to time. Most planning applications are dealt with properly. However, many people whose planning application is refused permission, fear some kind of conspiracy but, whereas councils can be inept, conspiracies are probably not nearly so common. Appeal decisions are less likely to be affected by non-planning considerations because inspectors, reporters and commissioners are independent and detached from the local scene. They give more objective decisions and are obliged to set out clearly their reasons for making them. If a non-planning factor influences a council's decision, it's not likely to admit this.

Since reasons for refusal have to be given in decision notices, the council will try to come up with planning reasons, no matter how feeble they appear. These are some considerations which on occasion affect planning decisions.

STRENGTH OF OPPOSITION

Objection to development from local residents isn't in itself a proper reason for refusing planning permission but is the most common reason why applications – which are acceptable in planning terms – are turned down by councils.

Councillors are politicians and susceptible to pressure from the local electorate. They want to make popular decisions, so weight of numbers can make a difference. Apart from the number of objections made, the identity of the objector can influence a result.

Parish councils don't decide planning applications but are consulted about them, and there's usually a close connection between parish and district councillors, both political and personal. District councillors can also be on the parish council and can be swayed by the parish council's objections. In a similar way, local amenity societies, residents groups, and various social organisations have links with councillors who might well be members themselves. Objections from these local groups sometimes seem to be given undue weight.

WHO YOU KNOW

Relationships between councillors and applicants do sometimes influence decisions. Personal contacts on the council allow either applicants or objectors to get their views across to the people who have the ultimate say. One or two councillors speaking forcefully for or against an application can change the course of a decision. The opposite effect also comes into play – if an applicant upsets a councillor or they dislike each other, the application is less likely to get a sympathetic hearing. At committee meetings, councillors who have a personal interest in an application are supposed to declare the fact and not take part in the decision. Interests can be financial, business, personal or any other relationship which could be seen to cause bias. The reputation of an applicant sometimes affects decisions – respected members of the community, or people with a record of successful development projects behind them, can get the benefit of any doubt while those who consistently offend the council or are believed to be unreliable, can suffer as a result.

OFFERING COMMUNITY BENEFITS

Occasionally, applicants have something of value to offer the council when they're making their planning application. This could be, for example, part of the site needed to complete a new public footpath, land suitable for a play area or other community facility or a ransom strip preventing access to other land. The benefit might not relate directly to the planning application but the council could take it into consideration nonetheless.

CORRUPTION

Individuals in councils sometimes accept offers of money or favours in return for their support but how much of this actually goes on is impossible to say. Accepting favours is a criminal offence and prosecutions are made from time to time, so the people involved obviously try to keep it quiet. Planning permission can add tens of thousands of pounds to the value of land, so the temptation will always be there.

CONSTRAINTS ON COUNCILS

There are sanctions that keep a check on councils and on wayward individuals within them. If a council refuses planning permission unreasonably, it faces the possibility of having to pay the applicant's costs of going to appeal. Complaints against councils are investigated by the

Local Government Ombudsman
(see Chapter 8) and compensation
can be paid. There's criminal law
enforcement in situations where
corruption takes place.

PART 2:

THE
APPLICATION

S ome people would say a planning application is just filling in a few
forms and sending them to the council with a drawing for approval.
That approach sometimes works but you'd be surprised at the
number of such people who end up with a notice of refusal, having
endured months of frustration and argument with the council. You'd
probably be more surprised to find out how simply the problems could
have been overcome – if the applicant had only understood the process
better. Planning permission means the difference between owning a
worthless piece of ground or a valuable building plot, or between staying
in your home or having to move. It's too important not to be dealt with
properly. Once you have a refusal, it's that much harder to get permission.
In this Part we look at what's involved in making planning applications, the
process they go through and what you can do to increase your chances of
getting planning permission.

CHAPTER 5

GETTING STARTED

More than 700,000 planning applications are currently made in the United Kingdom each year. Around 80 per cent are given permission. About 60 per cent of applications are for small building projects – extensions, alterations, loft conversions, single houses, or a few houses.

Planning applications comprise a completed form, ownership and agricultural certificates, location plan, drawings and, in many cases, a design and access statement and other reports/statements, plus whatever supporting material you want to submit, such as a letter or statement. We'll look at each of these in detail. Your planning application will be decided by the district council and the formal process the application goes through is shown in Figure 5.2 on page 44.

Once the application is submitted, there are often opportunities for taking action to influence the decision, which we'll study later. But the submission of an application should never be the start of the process of getting planning permission. Careful preparation is the key to success and time spent in the early stages is usually well rewarded.

Your starting point should be to decide exactly what you want to do. You might have to negotiate and modify your scheme later, but you need some firm ideas at the outset. If your project is a new house, work out what size it needs to be, how many floors you want and what sort of style. If your project is an extension, establish where you want it, what size you need and what it would look like. Sketch your ideas on paper (as in Figure 5.1 below) or get a sketch scheme drawn up for you.

Once you know what you want, the next step is to decide whether to get help in making your planning application, or whether to do it all yourself. This is for you

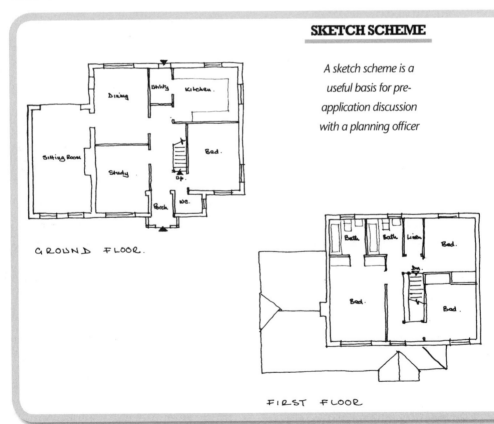

SKETCH SCHEME

A sketch scheme is a useful basis for pre-application discussion with a planning officer

GROUND FLOOR.

FIRST FLOOR

to judge but planning application requirements and the process are now so complicated that it's very hard for lay people to make their own applications. There's nothing to stop you doing some of the work involved or project managing the application, buying in help where needed.

Unless you're familiar with technical drawing and design, you'll, at least, need to get application drawings prepared.

REAR.

FRONT.

Figure 5.1

You can always try making a start yourself and call in other help if things get complicated at a later stage. Here are some suggestions for the sort of situations where you might benefit from professional help:

■ importance – where there's a lot at stake in terms of money or the enjoyment of your property;

■ complexity – where there are difficult planning laws or policy questions, previous refusals or specialist reports required;

■ time – where you're too busy or not available during the week;

■ cost – where you can afford to have someone to take on the work and the not always happy task of dealing with councils.

There are a number of professionals you can turn to. Building designers, for example architects, building surveyors and architectural technicians, can help define your requirements, prepare application drawings, make straightforward applications and advise on building costs.

Planning consultants can advise on how best to get permission, on planning rules and procedure and the chances of success, and they can also make applications and often arrange for your application

PLANNING APPLICATION PROCEDURE

APPLICANT

*Prepares planning application
and sends to the council*

VALIDATION/ADMINISTRATION

*Officer checks and registers application or requests further
documents, assigns to a planning officer, puts copy on deposit
for public and publishes on website, notifies neighbours, sends
copies to consultees*

GENERAL PUBLIC

*Neighbours and members of the
public send comments to the
council*

CONSULTEES

*Council departments, parish council,
highway/drainage authorities,
government bodies and others
respond to the council*

PLANNING OFFICER

*Studies application, inspects site, considers
general public and consultee comments, writes
report with recommendation*

DELEGATED DECISION

*Senior officer(s) considers and
endorses or changes report,
makes decision (without
referring to Planning Committee)*

COMMITTEE DECISION

*Councillors sent officer's report
prior to meeting, committee
discusses application and votes
on recommendation*

DECISION NOTICE

*Officer sends decision to applicant, records
decision in council records*

Note

*Planning applications in Northern Ireland are made to the Divisional Planning Office, assessed by a development
control officer and decided by the Divisional Planning Manager after consultation with the district council*

Figure 5.2

Applications go through a standard procedure although each council has its little quirks

drawings to be prepared too.

Many people automatically turn to their solicitor, because planning appears legalistic, yet very few solicitors are familiar with planning. Some larger estate agents offer planning services but check that they employ specialist planning professionals before using them.

You might hear of a 'friend-of-a-friend' who supposedly knows something about planning or who knows someone on the council – be very careful before trusting an important planning application to such a person.

Whoever you use, check their qualifications and experience, and make sure they're going to listen to you and do what you want. Some architects, for example, are renowned for taking their own independent line, so consider asking to speak to their former clients for a reference.

CHAPTER 6
INITIAL PREPARATION

Once you have a good idea of what you want to build and what professional help you're going to get, the next step is to prepare the ground for your planning application.

PRE-APPLICATION MEETING WITH A PLANNING OFFICER

To test the waters at an early stage, you can seek a meeting with a planning officer for an initial discussion. This can also help to firm-up your ideas. Where your project is a small-scale or very simple one, an initial meeting probably isn't necessary but for most projects, a pre-application meeting is usually worthwhile. When you're using consultants, they can meet the planning officer or attend the meeting with you. Many councils are quite open to holding meetings but there are various approaches to dealing with pre-application consultation. Some don't offer this service at all, others have formal systems with relatively simple forms to fill in, some ask you to write or send drawings for their comment instead of meeting, others have a duty planning officer system where an officer is available at certain times for callers. The planning section of councils' websites usually explain their pre-application advice procedure and set out the situations where a fee might be payable. Responses to written requests can take weeks, whereas a meeting gets an instant response, although that response could be less considered. The main purpose of a pre-application meeting with a planning officer is to identify any likely problems with the scheme that you want to build, so that you can deal with them before you submit your application. This is different from finding out the planning officer's ideal scheme for your site, which can happen if you don't take the initiative and go in with some positive ideas. Never go to such a meeting and just ask what the planning officer wants to see, as there's a danger of the officer's views getting entrenched behind his preferred type of development.

To arrange a meeting, phone the district council and ask to speak to a planning officer who deals with the area where the property is

located. The meeting could be held either at the council's offices or on site. See what the officer says, but it's usually easier to explain your proposals, and for the officer to assess them, in context at the site. Take your sketch scheme to the meeting to provide the basis for the discussion, although you don't need to give the officer a copy at this stage. There are occasions when it's better not to have your initial ideas on the planning department's file, as they could be used against you later. Describe briefly what you want to do but don't go into great detail about the project or explain all the personal circumstances behind it. First, the officer is only interested in the physical impact of the work and, second, you can very easily give something away that could count against you when the application is submitted. For example, if you eventually want to build two houses on a site but are initially applying for only one, the officer's views might be coloured unfavourably by the prospect of two houses being built, rather than just the one actually proposed.

At the meeting ask the planning officer to confirm the council's requirements for the content of the application and whether the council would require any specialists' reports. Council's have lists of reports and statements that might be required and these are on the council's website or available at the planning department. It's a good idea to have a copy to hand and run through the list with the officer, checking which are necessary, clarifying the level of detail appropriate to your proposal and finding out what sort of consultants you might need to help you. Also ask whether financial contributions would have to be made to the council in connection with your type of project, how the council deals with these and for confirmation of the amount(s) of money (see Chapter 7).

THE PLANNING OFFICER'S COMMENTS

Most planning officers give practical advice at pre-application meetings and you can chat amicably with them. If the officer is very negative or doesn't have a helpful attitude, try not to get into an argument – it's better to bite your lip than to create a hostile relationship at the outset. The unfortunate truth is that you need the planning officer's co-operation, but he or she doesn't need anything from you. Take full notes at the meeting, as these could be useful later. The planning officer will say whether he thinks you need to make a planning application, if there was any doubt, and can clarify what rights you might be able to take advantage of under the 'permitted development' rules noted in Part One. If you're told a planning application isn't necessary, you should at least ask for written confirmation and discuss with the officer whether to make a lawful development certificate application (see Chapter 2). The planning officer should be able to tell you if there are relevant planning policies and ask for the reference of any policies mentioned – title of the document, section and policy number. Some councils publish design guidance for new houses, extensions and other work, so find out if there's anything available that might help in your case. The officer should also say if the property is affected by any special planning designations (see Chapter 4) and you should ask what the effect of any such designation would be on your proposal and where you could look up more information about them. The planning officer should point out site-specific factors that will be weighed up when the application is made but bear in mind, unless the meeting takes place on site or you take a comprehensive set of photographs along to the meeting, the officer might not know of all the site's circumstances and features. Here are some examples:

■ natural features – trees, hedges and ground slope;

■ obstructions – overhead cables, telegraph poles and other structures;

■ existing buildings – design, layout and position on site;

■ adjoining buildings – relationship between buildings, position of windows, sizes and design;

■ access – highway safety and effect on environment;

■ plot – size, shape and relationship with other plots.

Earlier planning applications could have been made for development on your site – some you might know about but others could have been made by previous owners. The planning officer should have looked up the planning history before the meeting but check that this has been done. The officer

PLANNING RECORD CARD

TREADCARE DISTRICT COUNCIL

LAND EAST OF HOMELEA, CHURCH LANE

Total number of records found: 7

Ref no	Description	Decision	Appeal
126/62	Use of land as caravan site	Granted 1/7/63	
485/65	Erection of office/ toilets	Granted 4/11/65	
87/75	Extension for office	Granted 9/3/75	
983/87	Outline, 1 bungalow	Refused 12/2/87	Dismissed 8/2/88
95/00412/FP	Change of use to workshop	Granted 18/7/95	
04/0056/OUT	Outline,1 bungalow	Refused 3/6/04	Allowed 2/3/05
06/01107/FP	Erection of two detached houses	Granted 9/9/06	

Figure 6.1

District councils keep records of all planning decisions on computer or on cards, usually with a separate record for each property

might bring to the meeting the planning record card or computer printout for the site, listing all applications and decisions that have been made. If so, note the reference numbers of any decisions for similar proposals (an example of a record card is given in Figure 6.1 on the previous page). It's always useful to know how other planning applications have been decided by the council, and the planning officer should be able to refer you to similar proposals locally and tell you what decisions were made. Get the addresses and, if possible, application reference numbers of any comparable sites that are mentioned.

Having looked at your proposals and considered some of the issues, the planning officer should be in a position to say whether you're likely to get planning permission. Some planning officers are more reticent than others, however. Alternatively, the officer might suggest changes which would make the project more acceptable to the council or point out other action you could take before finalising the application. Many categories of planning application can be decided by planning officers, without going to a committee (delegated decisions) so find out if this could be the case for your application. Even if you take notes at the meeting, it can be worth asking the planning officer to confirm his views in writing, especially when the comments are positive. Bear in mind, though, that planning officers are usually much more cautious about what they put in writing than say at meetings. Even so, planning officers sometimes say things in letters they come to regret later but which you can use to your advantage. You might also be surprised by the difference in tone between the friendly chat you had face to face and the officious letter that arrives afterwards but this is quite normal. An example of a letter following a pre-application meeting is given in Figure 6.2.

If you decide to make changes in response to the officer's comments or in the light of your further research, arrange another pre-application meeting to go over amended drawings and ensure there were no misunderstandings about what the officer said. It's in your interests to try to get the proposal into a form you know the officer will support when the

PLANNING OFFICER LETTER

LOUGHBRIDGE DISTRICT COUNCIL

Our ref VT/BO/30
30th March 2009

Mr & Mrs R Cheerie
10 Granite Drive
Strathern
Monarch SH3 28P

Dear Mr & Mrs Cheerie

PROPOSED DWELLING — RANNOCKBURN ROAD, STRATHERN

I refer to your meeting with Mr Vince Tidyman of my department on 14th March 2009 and would comment as follows.

Whilst your proposal for a new dwelling at this site may be considered generally acceptable in principle, there are still some points of concern and, therefore, the proposal as it stands is not in an acceptable form.

The position of the garage would be close to principal windows of habitable rooms in the adjoining house which would adversely affect the amenities of occupants, and I suggest you consider whether the garage could be sited on the other side of the proposed house. The proposed dwelling is set back some distance into the site in relation to adjacent dwellings which may well give rise to mutual overlooking and would, therefore, represent an unneighbourly form of development.

At the front of the site there is an ash and an oak of some merit to the character and visual amenities of the area. The access drive and turning area pass very close to these trees and may affect their root systems. In conjunction with the re-positioning of the garage, you may wish to consider realigning the drive to take it farther away from these trees.

Please note that the points made in this letter are my informal comments and do not prejudice any future decision the council may make. If you want to discuss the proposal further, contact my planning officer, Mr Vince Tidyman.

Yours sincerely

Gordon McNeet

Director of Planning

Figure 6.2

Planning officers respond to pre-application enquiries by letter or email giving their initial opinions on draft proposals

application is made. Do remember that for delegated decisions, it's the officers who will actually decide the application.

JUDGING THE PLANNING OFFICER'S COMMENTS

You now know the planning officer's initial reaction to your project. It could be positive, negative or non-committal but, how much weight should you attach to his or her comments? The first and most important point is that what the planning officer says, in writing or verbally, doesn't commit the council in any way so it's not safe to take action or spend money based solely on what an officer tells you. It's the council's planning committee or, in the case of delegated decisions, senior officers who decide applications. Although committees are advised by officers, they can, and frequently do, go against that advice. In planning departments there's a hierarchy of officers (see Figure 6.3 on the opposite page). The views of junior members of the department are frequently overruled by senior officers – this is something to be wary of before relying too heavily on planning officers' initial comments. The more senior the officers are, the more negative their attitudes often seem to be and an initially positive reaction can become outright rejection. Senior officers check some letters and approve reports to committee and this can account for the difference between what you're told at a meeting and what's said in letters or what decision is made. The frustration is often compounded by officers' subsequent back-peddling from what they said in the first place.

Planning officers are supposed to give impartial advice to the public but remember, they're employees of the council, not independent advisers and their judgement and advice can be coloured by various factors. Officers are constrained by council policy and while they might feel, on the merits of the particular case, that your proposal is acceptable, it could still conflict with council policy. Unfortunately, the latter usually prevails over common sense. If you fear this is happening, ask the officer to say specifically what harm your proposal would cause and make a note of the answer. Where there's doubt over whether a planning application is needed at

DISTRICT COUNCIL PLANNING DEPARTMENT PERSONNEL

DIRECTOR OF PLANNING

DEPUTY DIRECTOR OF PLANNING

POLICY	ADMINISTRATION	DEVELOPMENT CONTROL	
Head of policy		Head of development control	
Senior planning officer	Team leader	Western area	Eastern area
Senior planning officer	Validation officer	Team leader	Team leader
Senior planning officer	Validation officer	Senior planning officer	Senior planning officer
		Senior planning officer	Senior planning officer
Planning officer	Technician		
Planning officer	Technician	Planning officer	Planning officer
		Planning officer	Planning officer
Economic development officer	Admin support	Planning assistant	Planning assistant
Planning assistant		Enforcement officer	Enforcement officer
		Tree officer	Conservation officer

Figure 6.3

District council planning departments are arranged in teams and hierarchies and it's often useful to know what level of officer you're dealing with

all, planning officers will normally say permission is required. They do this for two main reasons. First, councils like to keep as much power over development as they can and, if their permission isn't needed, they have no control – they can't refuse it, insist on amendments or attach conditions. Second, councils collect fees from applicants for planning applications and every application made represents another fee.

To assess the officer's advice and to help form your own view, look up the planning policies, especially any mentioned by the planning officer at a meeting, on the council's website. The district council planning department keeps copies of all relevant documents which you can study or buy copies to take away, although they're often expensive. The planning department has receptionists to help you; generally they're knowledgeable but they're not qualified planning officers. Ask them for policy documents and any guidance, booklets or leaflets that could help. Look up the relevant sections of the policy documents and the planning policies you noted at the meeting, and read the accompanying text which explains

the policies. See whether your project complies, bearing in mind what the officer said about the policy in relation to your proposal. Find your site on the proposals map, which comes with the policy document, to see how the area is designated (countryside, settlement, Conservation Area, etc – see Figure 6.4 opposite for an example). Look at the policies that apply to the designation and make notes, so that you can quote the policies in your planning application.

While you're at the planning department, look up any other planning applications referred to by the officer. Many councils put application documents on their websites and you can research and see them there. These could be previous decisions on your site or other decisions in the area. You're allowed to see the papers on all planning applications, not just for your own site, once they've been decided. The most important documents to find are:

■ application forms and drawings;
■ planning officer's report;
■ council's decision notice;
■ inspector's appeal decision, if there was an appeal.

Reading these should give you a good idea of the sort of

Figure 6.4

Proposals maps show policies that apply to certain areas and define development boundaries

issues that come up and how the council will assess them when your application is considered. Make a note of points that seem useful or apply to your case or buy photocopies of the documents. Don't presume that, just because other applications were granted or refused, your application will be decided the same way, as each case should be looked at on its merits. Planning decisions, however, are supposed to be fair and consistent. If you're not clear about anything you see in the policy documents or in other planning applications, ask to speak to a planning officer who should be able to clarify the points.

OTHER PRE-APPLICATION CONTACTS

When your planning application is made, the council has to consult other bodies and other council departments. Who's consulted depends on what the application is for, so ask the planning officer who would be consulted on your particular type of proposal. Standard consultees for new housing are the drainage authority and the highway authority. The latter is either the district council itself or, in most non-unitary authority areas, the county council. Other consultees include conservation, environmental health or rights of way officers, Environment Agency, parish council and other local interest groups. It's sometimes worth speaking to consultees before you make your application. Your meeting with the planning officer and your research at the planning department should alert you to potential problems which are relevant to a consultee. A phone call to the district council will get you the names and addresses, or contact details should be available via the council's website. Some typical highway and drainage problems that arise are:

■ location of access points;
■ complying with technical standards for access;
■ providing adequate visibility splays at access points;
■ ability of roads to take additional vehicles;
■ location of public sewers;
■ capacity of sewers;
■ suitability of site for private sewage treatment plant.

If you have doubts over these aspects, contact the authorities directly. Most have departments that deal with planning consultations and generally their staff are prepared to comment. Try telephoning first to discuss your query, as they might be able to put your mind at rest straight away or, alternatively, they'll ask you to write, perhaps sending a plan or arrange to meet you on site (an example of a letter to a highway authority is given in Figure 6.5 opposite). See what they say and ask how to overcome any potential problems they raise. If you can reach agreement with the authority, get this confirmed in writing. Planning departments work closely with other authorities and having something in writing should stop any behind-the-scenes manoeuvring when your application is submitted. If you can't reach agreement, think about getting help from a planning consultant or firm of consulting engineers. Your application is unlikely to succeed in the face of an objection from a highway or drainage authority.

LETTER TO HIGHWAY AUTHORITY BEFORE MAKING A PLANNING APPLICATION

County Surveyor and Engineer
Highways Department
County Hall
Ridgeborough
East Moorland
RO21 7EZ

5th April 2009

Dear Sir

PROPOSED DWELLING AT PLOT NEXT TO MERRYVALE COTTAGE, EASTINGS RIDE, NEWELL

Please find the enclosed location plan showing this site. We would be grateful if you could indicate whether forming a new access point onto Eastings Lane to serve a single dwelling would be acceptable to your authority.

There is an existing field gate near the western boundary which has been used for many years by agricultural vehicles to get access to the land and this point has good visibility along Eastings Lane.

Please can you also confirm our understanding that the group of small saplings in the verge are within the public highway and can be removed to provide clear visibility.

If you have questions or would like more information, please contact me.

Yours faithfully

G Pleasant

Graham & Julie Pleasant

Figure 6.5

You can write to the highway authority to find out whether it will accept your proposed access and parking and turning areas

Since district councillors are ultimately responsible for deciding planning applications, you can contact them before making your application. There's nothing wrong in doing this, as councillors are elected to help their constituents (although dealing with the planning officer is sufficient in most instances). However, councils have different policies on lobbying and some discourage it, so check with the planning department first. At this early stage, councillors might in any case refer you back to the planning officers, and lobbying councillors is generally best left until later, when the application is actually under way. But, if your initial meetings with the officer didn't go well, if you know your application might be controversial or if you happen to know a councillor, an early chat could help your application. If you don't know who your local councillors are, contact the district council or look on the council's website where you'll find councillors' names, contact addresses, the wards they represent and the committees on which they sit. Most councils produce year books listing the same information. Councillors' grasp of planning is variable but many who serve on the planning committee for a length of time become reasonably familiar with the types of proposal that succeed or fail, although they do rely on planning officers' expertise for professional appraisals of applications and technical advice. Their comments could well help but you shouldn't rely on them, as councillors might be reluctant to offend you by saying your application should be refused and that they'll oppose it. There'll be 10 to 20 councillors on the planning committee and, while support from one or two local councillors can make a difference, they still have to convince the remaining members.

You can also contact parish councillors, whose views on an application don't have to be followed but, in some cases, they're given disproportionate weight by district councils. Parish councillors' grasp of the subtleties of the planning system can be minimal but all the points made about contacting district councillors are relevant to contacting parish councillors. Both residents groups and local amenity societies can influence planning decisions so, if your application could be of wider interest than to immediate neighbours, think about discussing it with these groups. The planning officer can tell you which local organisations comment on applications. Some are interested in local architecture and history so, if your property is in a Conservation Area or involves a Listed Building, try discussing it with them. Of course, contacting these sorts of groups could be counter-productive – if they don't like what you propose, it will give them time to organise their objections.

The main source of opposition to planning applications is neighbours, because people are sensitive about changes in their immediate area and sometimes neighbours are offended when proposals aren't mentioned to them before a planning application is made. Your neighbours (or prospective neighbours) will be notified by the council in any event so, if you have a reasonable relationship with them, speak to them at an early stage. Think which properties could be affected, see what your neighbours have to say, and if possible, agree compromises with them. Approaching adjoining owners you don't know is more difficult and there might be some natural suspicion to overcome. If you're not currently living at the property, possibly try writing to the neighbours first. It's important to win as many people to your side as possible.

CHAPTER 7

PREPARING THE PLANNING APPPLICATION

You've now got the planning officer's initial reaction and, if necessary, you've spoken to consultees, decided whether you need to speak to anyone else about your proposals, ascertained what information will have to be submitted with the application and, maybe, you've revised the project in the light of these contacts – you're now ready to prepare a planning application. In England, the government specifies mandatory requirements for the content of all applications and individual councils then specify their particular additional requirements in what is usually referred to as a 'local list' or 'validation checklist'. These requirements will be on the council's website or available at its offices and have to be met in order for the application to be validated and processed. However, which documents from the local list the council will actually want depends on the exact nature and circumstances of an application. If you didn't confirm the council's requirements for your proposal with a planning officer during previous pre-application discussion, speak to a person in the planning department who validates applications and try to agree which documents will be required.

TYPES OF PLANNING APPLICATION:
FULL AND OUTLINE APPLICATIONS

We saw in Chapter 1 that there are two basic types of planning application – full and outline (application in principle in Scotland) – with full applications showing all the details of a proposal, and outline applications establishing the principle of new building, leaving some or all details (layout, scale, external appearance, access and landscaping) to be approved later. Most planning applications for domestic development are made in full, although there are some situations where it's better to make an outline application – for example, if you want to sell your property and make an application to establish value or maximise value, an outline is normally sufficient as it allows purchasers to apply for the type of building they want in a reserved matters application. Outline is also useful

where you're uncertain whether planning permission will be given, as you don't need full drawings of the proposal, although you can put in illustrations – this saves on work and expense. When outline applications are made, the council has the right to ask for further details but this is only done in exceptional circumstances where design and layout are important factors in deciding whether to give permission at all. In Conservation Areas, councils usually insist on full applications. If a site already has full planning permission this doesn't stop you making another full planning application. However, if you apply for a house in a different position, the council might be worried that two houses could be built and ask for your agreement to revoke the earlier permission.

A fee must be paid to the council for making planning applications (see Planning Application Fees on pages 81–84). The level of fee for new houses and flats varies and is dependent on whether the application is full or outline. Fees for outline applications are calculated on the area of the site and a further fee is paid when the reserved matters are submitted, whereas fees for full applications are based just on the number of houses or flats to be created. This means outline/reserved matters applications cost more than full applications, especially for larger application sites, that is, those over 0.1 hectare/0.25 acres.

RESERVED MATTERS APPLICATIONS

After outline permission is granted, the details of the scheme can be put forward in a reserved matters application, which can be made using a planning application form but doesn't have to be. A simple letter is all that is required identifying the site, the approved proposal and the council's reference number and date of the outline permission, together with the drawings described later in this chapter. Reserved matters applications must be submitted within three years of the date when outline planning permission was granted. Any number of different reserved matters can be put forward on the same outline permission but only one scheme can be built. Anyone can make a reserved matters application and it doesn't have to be made by the person who obtained the outline permission. The details shown in

a reserved matters application must be consistent with the original outline permission and any conditions which were attached to it. So, for example, with an outline permission for a bungalow, you can't show a two-storey house in the reserved matters application.

Even where outline permission has been given, there's nothing to stop you making a completely new planning application for full permission, instead of a reserved matters application. Do this where you want to amend the proposal outside the scope of the outline permission, perhaps including a different site area or different form of development or, if the three-year time period for making the reserved matters application has nearly expired, as a full permission gives you another three years to begin the development. On the other hand, where a council grants outline permission reluctantly or it's won on appeal, there can be an advantage to submitting reserved matters rather than a new application – with a new application the council is entitled to look again at the whole proposal, rather than just the design and layout.

RENEWAL OF PLANNING PERMISSION

Planning permission can be renewed in two circumstances: first, where full permission has been granted but isn't carried out or begun within three years, or where a reserved matters application hasn't been made within three years of an outline permission; and second, where permission is granted for only a limited period. The latter is unusual for domestic development but could relate to uses such as part business use or for a mobile home, where the council might allow a trial period or recognise a temporary need for something it wouldn't permit permanently. To renew a permission that hasn't been carried out or begun, you have to submit a new planning application. There is, however, a simplified application process you can use for this which includes identifying the original permission and payment of an application fee. Make sure you apply before the original permission expires – leave yourself a good few months if possible. If the new application is refused, this should leave you time to get all the conditions approved and start

work in order to keep the previous permission alive. We'll look later at what work constitutes the beginning of development (see Chapter 8). An application made to renew a permission shouldn't be refused by the council unless there's been a material change in circumstances. This could include physical circumstances, like other new buildings having been built or changes in the council's planning policies, such as a new Local Development Framework or Local Plan coming into force or a Conservation Area being designated. Even if you miss the chance to renew a permission, the fact that it was granted relatively recently is still an important part of the planning history of a site. There should be good reason to justify refusing another similar application, so make a new planning application as soon as it's possible to do so. Where there's a time-limited planning permission, you can make a completely new application, or apply to vary or remove the condition that imposes the time limit. Usually it's best to change the condition, and although such an application can still be turned down, the council should consider only the effect of the condition, and not the whole scheme. Make the application before the time limit expires and discuss with the planning officer whether there's a continuing need for the permission to be on a temporary basis – if the condition is removed completely, it won't be necessary for you to keep on re-applying.

REMOVING OR VARYING CONDITIONS

Conditions not only make planning permission temporary, many other aspects of development can also be controlled by conditions. Some need to be complied with before or during the construction, such as demolishing an existing building or forming an access, while other conditions continue to have effect after the building is built, such as maintaining landscaping schemes or preventing any new window openings. Circumstances can change over time, or you could find a condition is too restrictive. There are three ways to deal with this:
■ ignore the condition and see what happens;
■ appeal against the condition, within six months;
■ make a planning application to remove or vary the condition.

The right answer depends on the specific circumstances of each case. For example, ignoring a condition that restricts construction work on a new building to between 8.00 am and 5.00 pm on weekdays, isn't going to land you in serious trouble if you decide to do some plastering or painting at the weekend. But councils do have powers to make you comply with conditions and you could find yourself having to alter work already done or being fined in the magistrates' court for more serious contravention of conditions. When permission is granted, you can appeal straight away against conditions you don't like but the danger here is that inspectors can overrule the decision to grant permission, not just the conditions. If the condition is significant and unacceptable, it's best to apply to remove it from the permission. Read the original decision notice to find out why the council included the condition, look at a copy of the planning officer's report to committee at the planning department to see what's said about the need for the condition there and discuss all your objections to the condition with the planning officer.

If the permission is recent and circumstances haven't changed, the council could be reluctant to remove conditions, but if you can point to changes in circumstances or make a good case, you might be able to persuade the council either to remove or vary the conditions. Where you think you might need to appeal, it's best to go ahead with an application, even though you know it'll be refused. In an appeal against a council's refusal to remove or vary a condition, the inspector can't overturn the original permission.

PLANNING APPLICATION FORMS

The first thing you need is a set of forms and guidance notes, obtainable from the district council website or planning department. In England and Northern Ireland standard forms are common to all council/divisional office areas. In England and Wales applications can be made on-line via the Planning Portal website. Scottish councils can now accept on-line applications via ePlanning Scotland. Read the guidance notes before completing the forms and taking photocopies. Don't put a date on the application until it's ready for submission. Planning application forms vary between UK countries but similar questions are asked by all of them. The section headings of the standard form for England are set out in Figure 7.1 on the next page. The forms provide the council with the information on which your proposal is assessed and decided, and we now look at the factors to consider when answering the main questions.

APPLICANT

The applicant is the person who makes the planning application but he or she doesn't need to own or occupy all, or even part, of the property. If you make a planning application on someone else's property, you must notify the owner (see Notices and Certificates on pages 78–81). Planning permission relates to the application site not to the applicant. This allows you to get planning permission and sell the property with the benefit of permission, or to buy a property which already has planning permission and use that permission. One person's name is usually sufficient on the form but, if the property is owned by more than one person, you should choose between either putting all

**PLANNING APPLICATION
SECTION HEADINGS**

*Applicant name, address and contact
   details*
*Agent name, address and contact
   details*
Description of proposal
Address details
Pre-application advice
*Pedestrian and vehicle access, roads
   and rights of way*
Waste storage and collection
*Neighbour and community
   consultation*
Council employee/member
Materials
Vehicle parking
Foul sewage
Assessment of flood risk
*Biodiversity and geological
   conservation*
Existing use
Trees and hedges
Residential units
Site area
Site visit
Certificates
Declaration

*Planning application forms require you to
provide information under these main section
headings (based on English forms)*

Figure 7.1

the names on the form or giving
the other owners notice of the
application. The decision you make
depends on convenience and on
whether the application is being
made jointly by all owners. One
point to note at this stage is that
only the person who makes an
application can appeal against
refusal of planning permission or
against conditions. The address
and phone number you give
doesn't have to be your home, so
put the address where you can
be contacted most easily and give
a phone number where you can
be contacted during office hours.
Whatever address and number
you give is likely to be picked up
by contractors and suppliers of
building products, who'll send you
their literature or phone you.

AGENT

Where you use consultants they
should complete the forms or at
least check them for you before
they're submitted. Where your
consultants are making the
application, ask them to send
you a draft to double-check and
approve. Your consultants will
put their name and address on
the form and the council will
correspond directly with them.

DESCRIPTION OF THE DEVELOPMENT

This is probably the most important question on the form as the description largely governs what you'll have permission to do. Be as concise and accurate as possible – there's no need to specify every last detail of your proposal (see Figure 7.2 below). Applicants can sometimes shoot themselves in the foot by listing exhaustively all the items of work – including internal work (which

EXAMPLES OF GOOD AND BAD DESCRIPTIONS

GOOD	BAD
Erection of dwelling and garage	4 bed, one with en suite bathroom, 5 reception, two-storey cottage-style house, double garage with pitched roof, gravel drive and turning area and landscaped gardens
Erection of extension and alterations to existing building	New utility room, addition to dining room and fourth bedroom, re-fit kitchen and move sink, add dormer window with pitched roof and tile hanging, strip and re-tile hang first floor rear
Change of use from agriculture to residential garden	Part arable field next to side of garden 40m x 20m to be used as general purpose garden with lawn, shrub beds, fruit trees, sheds play equipment and garden refuse area
Conversion of barn to single dwelling	Work to semi-derelict timber frame farm building to make modern executive unit, involving side extension, additional windows to light roof space, possible future conversion of cart shed to form pool house and possible pool area

Figure 7.2

Over-elaborate descriptions of your proposed development in a planning application form can cause confusion and create the wrong impression, so keep it simple

doesn't even need permission) and future work not immediately proposed – which makes the proposal sound far more extensive than it is. Planning officers and neighbours can be alarmed by the apparent scale of the work. If you're making a full application for a house, there's no need to say in the description how many bedrooms it has or what style it would be. Similarly, for an extension you don't need to say how all the new rooms will be used, as the application drawings should show all this information.

SITE ADDRESS

The normal postal address of the property is sufficient in most cases. The important point is that the council can identify where the site is and this becomes slightly more difficult when the property doesn't have its own address, possibly because there's no building currently there. You'll also be submitting a location plan and this helps.

Property without an address is usually described by phrases such as: 'Land west of London Road'; 'Site between Heather Down and Brambles, Parsonage Lane'; 'Land adjoining 26 Edwards Way'; or 'Plot rear of 6 & 7 James Street'. If the application is for a new house or houses, give the site its own address as in the examples. It's a small point, but it does start to sow the seed that the site in question is a separate entity and not part of an existing garden or field.

PRE-APPLICATION ADVICE

If you've had any discussions with officers – whether that's several meetings or just clarification of what information is required – give the name(s) of the officer and outline the nature of the advice. Remember that what ever pre-application advice you got it won't commit the council, so don't be tempted to over-egg any positive comments the officer made in the mistaken belief it will guarantee success.

ACCESS

The forms only ask whether you're altering or closing an access but councils set standards for access and turning areas, with which your scheme will have to comply, covering:

■ types of road where direct access points are allowed;

■ numbers of houses which

various categories of road can take;

■ turning-heads for vehicles;
■ visibility at access points;
■ turning areas within sites.

The planning department can tell you the council's requirements – comply with them if you can or, if not, try to negotiate an acceptable compromise. Providing visibility splays at access points can cause problems if all the land involved isn't owned by you or within the public highway, or contains obstacles. You must be able to show that visibility splays can be created and kept permanently clear. This sometimes means buying strips of land or arranging for obstacles such as bushes or walls to be moved. Most new houses involve forming an access

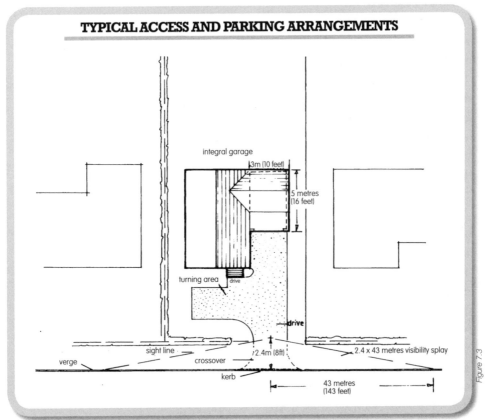

TYPICAL ACCESS AND PARKING ARRANGEMENTS

integral garage
3m (10 feet)
5 metres (16 feet)
turning area   drive
drive
sight line   2.4m (8ft)   2.4 x 43 metres visibility splay
verge   crossover
kerb
43 metres (143 feet)

Figure 7.3

Highway authorities have standards for access and parking arrangements with which you'll be expected to comply and providing a turning area on site for cars. If your access is shared and/or owned partly by someone else, remember that it all needs to be edged in red on the location plan, and that you'll also have to notify the other owner of your application. Typical access and parking arrangements are shown in Figure 7.3 on page 69.

WASTE STORAGE

You have to state and show on your drawings where rubbish and recycling bins can be kept. This is an issue councils take seriously although isn't usually a problem for single dwellings. Meeting council requirements for bin storage can become an issue in applications for flats – conversion or new build – especially where space is limited.

NEIGHBOUR CONSULTATION

We looked at speaking to neighbours or the parish council (see Chapter 6) and where you've done this you can say so on the form. If the consultations were extensive or involved, set out what you did and the results in a separate document and refer to that in the form. Otherwise state who you spoke to and summarise their responses.

MATERIALS

The form asks about existing and proposed external materials and finishes. When your project is an extension or alterations you can complete this fully and the council is likely to expect matching or complementary materials. The latter might be contrasting materials where this works in design terms. For new builds there are obviously no existing materials to enter on the form, and for outline applications you might not know at the application stage what materials you want.

PARKING

Councils have standards for the number of parking spaces for different dwelling types and for the dimensions of parking and disabled spaces. The numbers of spaces specified are supposed to be maximums rather than minimums, in line with government guidance to cut down on car use but, in practice, councils tend to discourage providing less than their standards. Aim to meet the standard or, if that's not possible, explain in your application why this is impractical and/or unnecessary, for example because the property is in a town centre or close to a station or bus stop with regular services. Extensions, alterations and buildings in the grounds could take up parking spaces, but try to make sure the council's standard can still be met.

DRAINAGE

There are two types of drainage – foul drainage and surface water. Foul drainage caters for sinks, baths, toilets and washing machines and goes to the nearest public sewer or, if there's no sewer, to a private treatment plant on the site. Surface water is rain and is dealt with under the flood risk heading (opposite). The form asks what drainage method is proposed and whether it's an existing system. With existing houses you'll have a drainage system in place and, in most cases, any new sanitary fittings can be connected up to the existing system, subject to capacity. Your builder, building surveyor or designer should be able to tell you whether the existing system is adequate.

For new homes, establish the drainage method before you make the application (see Part Four). A few councils are particularly fussy about drainage and ask for very detailed information when an application is submitted – get help from a drainage engineer or building surveyor if you have problems. Examples of different drainage connections are shown in Figure 7.4 on the next page.

FLOOD RISK

If your site or property is in an area at risk of flooding you might need advice from an engineer and to submit a Flood Risk Assessment (FRA) with the application. Flood risk areas are defined by the Environment Agency in England and Wales, the Scottish Environment Protection Agency, and the Rivers Agency in Northern Ireland. You can check with the relevant body whether your property falls within a flood risk zone. This can be done on their websites by entering the postcode. Risk of flooding can prevent planning permission being granted so it's something to establish early on in the process. You state in this section how surface water will be disposed of and the most common methods are public surface water drain in built-up areas, watercourse (ditch or stream) or to a soakaway on the site.

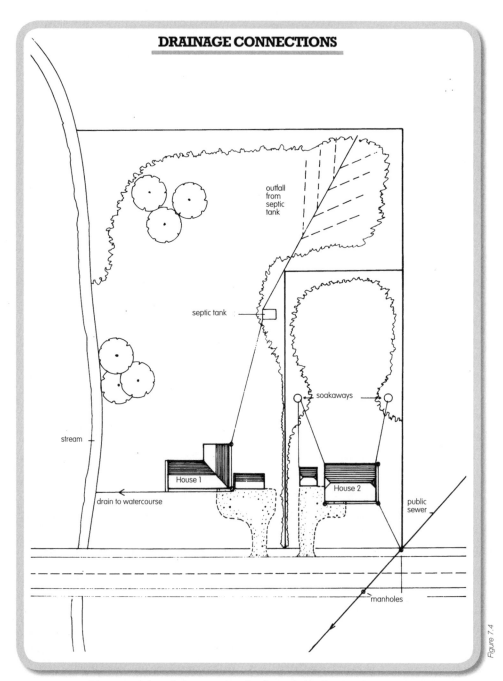

DRAINAGE CONNECTIONS

outfall from septic tank

septic tank

soakaways

stream

House 1

House 2

drain to watercourse

public sewer

manholes

Figure 7.4

There are various drainage options for disposal of foul and surface water

BIODIVERSITY AND GEOLOGICAL CONSERVATION

In plain language this translates to trees, plants and wildlife, and other natural features of the site, like rock formations. The council wants to know whether there are any protected species on the land, whether it has geological interest or whether it has any special designation, such as a SSSI (see Chapter 4). This is relatively rare but, if present, can necessitate a report by an ecologist or geologist to show that the wildlife or other features wouldn't be harmed by the build.

EXISTING USES

Where your application relates to an existing house, the use is residential and you need say no more than that. If your application is for a new house, it's best to put 'residential' as the existing use, because you're then dealing with the question of a building on land with residential use already established. You can do this where the plot is part of a garden or is in a residential estate. If the site isn't in residential use, describe it as 'vacant' if you can, to give the impression it doesn't have a beneficial use. Alternatively, if

there's an existing use taking place which has undesirable effects on the area, such as noise, smell or traffic dangers, state that use and make it sound as unpleasant as possible – granting planning permission for your proposal would get rid of it. There are questions about contamination and, where there this could be present, perhaps because of previous industrial or vehicle uses, you might have to get a survey and report carried out by a suitable consultant. Speak to the planning department if you're not sure about this.

TREES

You have to indicate whether there are trees or hedges on the development site itself, and whether there are any on adjoining sites that might be affected. This relates to trees rather than bushes and shrubs. If the proposal could have an effect on trees, the council might require a tree survey by an arboriculturist (tree expert). Such surveys establish the importance and health of trees and root protection zones – areas around valuable trees to be retained within which excavation should be avoided, or special measures taken to avoid root damage. Some (but not all) councils are prepared to exercise common sense and, providing no significant trees would be near any buildings, won't insist on a survey. Trees to be lost should be shown on your application drawings, as well as root protection zones. Avoid saying the number of trees to be lost, this information could be too easily seized on and used by objectors, regardless of the quality or value of the trees in question.

If there are trees on site protected by a Tree Preservation Order (TPO), try to avoid losing them or siting buildings too close. TPO trees aren't sacrosanct, however, so make an assessment of their health and importance and if necessary take advice from an arboriculturist. Unless a tree is protected by a TPO or is in a Conservation Area, there's nothing to stop you felling it before applying for permission, although many people are reluctant to do this, for understandable reasons. Unfortunately, councils sometimes use TPOs as a means to prevent development. This leaves the applicant either going to appeal with a proposal involving the

loss of TPO trees or trying to re-negotiate a restricted scheme with the council. An example of an application drawing showing trees lost is given in Figure 7.5 opposite.

RESIDENTIAL UNITS

Where the project involves creating new houses or flats – from a new single house to the sub-division of a building into flats – you have to give the number of existing and proposed units, the type of unit and the number of bedrooms in the units.

SITE AREA

The application site is the area around which you draw a red line on the location plan. This needn't be the whole of your property, although that's usually the most appropriate. The application site can include land that you don't own and for new houses councils usually ask for the red edging to include access to a public road. This can cause problems where access is gained via a length of private road as you would have to serve a notice of the application if you don't own all the private road. If you're in any doubt, ask a planning officer what to include within the site. Any land you own

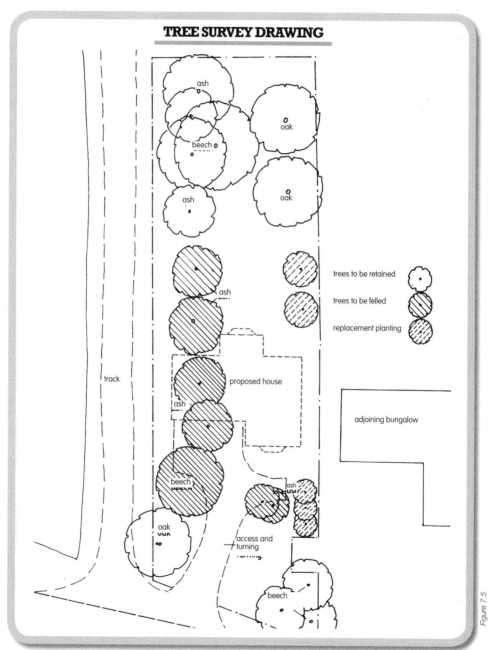

TREE SURVEY DRAWING

Where there are significant trees on or close to a site, the council will require a tree survey to be submitted with planning application

or control outside the application site should have a blue line drawn around it. Planning application fees for outline applications are calculated on the area of the site and, although councils don't always like it, it's sometimes possible to reduce the fee by

LOCATION PLANS

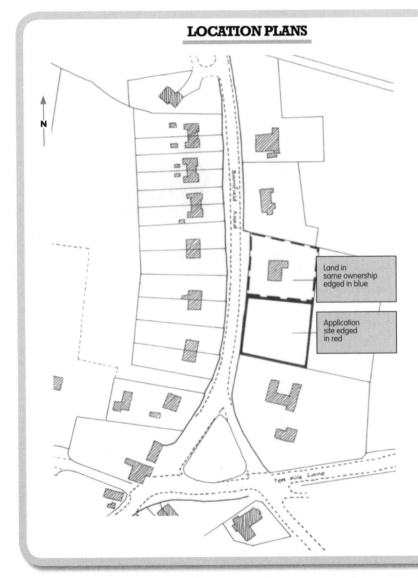

Land in same ownership edged in blue

Application site edged in red

N

Planning applications must include a location plan showing the site

excluding some of the land but you must include all land where work is to take place. If the site isn't already part of a garden or on a residential estate, you should include all areas that you would like to be used as garden. It's advisable to check the site area

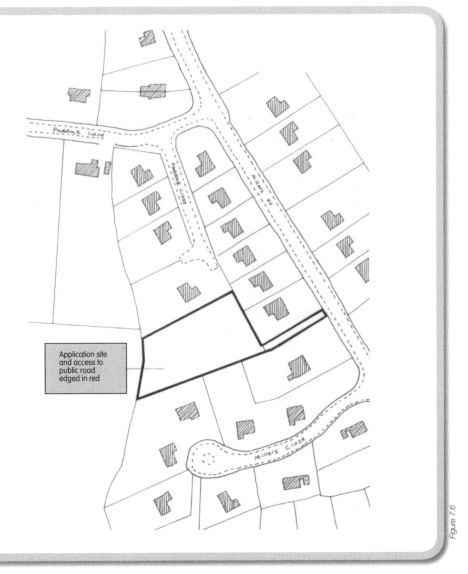

Application site and access to public road edged in red

Figure 7.6

edged in red and other land in the control of the applicant edged in blue

yourself as other sources, such as estate agents' particulars, or previous owners' calculations, might not be accurate. Examples of planning application location plans are given in Figure 7.6 on pages 76 and 77.

SITE VISIT

The planning officer will inspect the site at some point after the application is submitted. Mostly officers turn up unannounced regardless of what you say on the form but, where it's not possible to see the site or relevant part of it without someone being present, the officer will contact whoever you name on the form to make access arrangements. This can be your consultant or designer where you're using one, or some other person if it's not easy for you to attend.

NOTICES AND CERTIFICATES

All planning applications must be accompanied by certificates in which you state whether you own all the application site, whether anyone else owns some or all of the site and whether any of the site is part of an agricultural tenancy (even if it's in a city centre). These certificates are incorporated in the standard application forms. If you're not the owner or there's an agricultural tenancy, you must send a notice of the application to the owner or agricultural tenant. For these purposes, an owner includes tenants with seven years or more left on their lease. You need to complete one of four different certificates, depending on the circumstances:

■ Certificate A – the applicant is the only owner (see Figure 7.7 opposite);

■ Certificate B – someone else owns all or part of the site. The owner(s) name and address is shown on the certificate along with the date that notice of the application was sent to them (see Figure 7.8 on page 80);

■ Certificate C – the applicant can't find out the names and addresses of all owners after taking reasonable steps, including a newspaper advert. The steps taken, the name of the newspaper and the date of publication must be given;

■ Certificate D – the applicant can't find out the names and addresses of any owners. The requirements are the same as for certificate C.

An Agricultural Holdings Certificate

CERTIFICATE A

Town and Country Planning (General Development Procedure) Order 1995

CERTIFICATE UNDER ARTICLE 7

Certificate A

I certify that:

On the day 21 days before the date of the accompanying application nobody, except the applicant, was the owner of any part of the land to which the application relates.

Agricultural Holdings Certificate

None of the land to which the application relates is, or is part of, an agricultural holding.

Signed

Sylvia Passmore

On behalf of

Date   18 June 2009

(a) This Certificate is for use with applications and appeals for planning permission (articles 7 and 9(1) of the Order). One of Certificates A, B, C or D (or the appropriate certificate in the case of certain minerals applications) must be completed, together with the Agricultural Holdings Certificate.

(b) 'owner' means a person having a freehold interest or a leasehold interest the unexpired term of which is not less than seven years, or, in the case of development consisting of the winning and working of minerals, a person entitled to an interest in a mineral in the land (other than oil, gas, gold or silver).

Figure 7.7

Certificate A is submitted where the applicant is the sole owner of the whole application site

CERTIFICATE B

Town and Country Planning (General Development Procedure) Order 1995

CERTIFICATE UNDER ARTICLE 7

Certificate B
I certify that:
The applicant has given the requisite notice to everyone else who, on the day 21 days before the date of the accompanying application, was the owner of any part of the land to which the application relates, as listed below.

Owner's name	Address at which notice was served	Date on which notice was served
Jason Bone	Bluebriar Station Road Huntdown	30 May 2009

Agricultural Holdings Certificate
None of the land to which the application relates is, or is part of, an agricultural holding.
OR
~~I have/the applicant has/the appellant has* given the requisite notice to every person other than my/him/her* self who, on the day 21 days before the date of the application/appeal*, was a tenant of an agricultural holding on all or part of the land to which the application/appeal * relates, as follows:~~

~~Tenant's Name~~	~~Address at which notice notice was served~~	~~Date on which was served~~

Signed

Sylvia Passmore

On behalf of
Date   30 May 2009

(a) This Certificate is for use with applications and appeals for planning permission (articles 7 and 9(1) of the Order). One of Certificates A, B, C or D (or the appropriate certificate in the case of certain minerals applications) must be completed, together with the Agricultural Holdings Certificate.

(b) 'owner' means a person having a freehold interest or a leasehold interest the unexpired term of which is not less than seven years, or, in the case of development consisting of the winning and working of minerals, a person entitled to an interest in a mineral in the land (other than oil, gas, gold or silver).

Figure 7.8

Certificate B is submitted where the applicant isn't the sole owner of the whole application site states either the site isn't part of an agricultural tenancy or the name of the agricultural tenants and when a notice of the application was sent to them. This is usually incorporated in certificate A or B (see Figure 7.7 and 7.8 on pages 79-80).

In all but a very few cases, certificate A or B will be appropriate. To send a notice to owners or agricultural tenants, you fill in a standard form (see Figure 7.9 on page 82). The information you give includes details of the proposal as described in the application form, the address of the council and the date by which any comments must be made to the council – 21 days from when the notice is sent. You should send the notices to owners at the same time you make the application but you don't send a copy of the notice to the council.

The purpose of the notice is to let owners and tenants know about planning applications which affect their property. It's a statutory requirement, which means you still have to send a notice even when the application is made with the full knowledge and support of the owner. Unless you're in close contact with the owners or tenants, it's worth writing a covering letter to go with the notice, because some people panic on receiving an official notice. Write a pleasant letter saying briefly what's going on, and, most importantly, inviting them to contact you first, should they have questions or objections. It's far better for you to resolve these points than to have an objection made to the council. Certificates and notices are available from the same source as the application forms. If you have any doubts about which certificates or notices to submit or about completing them, contact the planning department.

PLANNING APPLICATION FEES

Most planning applications have to be accompanied by a fee – a cheque made payable to the council is the usual method of payment (even with on-line applications). Mistakes over fees are easily made although the Planning Portal website, covering England and Wales, includes a fee calculator which helps. The guidance notes, which come with the set of application forms, usually contain a schedule of current application fees, which

NOTICE OF A PLANNING APPLICATION

Town and Country Planning (General Development Procedure) Order 1995

NOTICE UNDER ARTICLE 6 OF APPLICATION FOR PLANNING PERMISSION
(to be published in a newspaper or to be served on an owner* or a tenant**)

Proposed development at:	**Land adjoining The Blue Pearl, Bootlace Lane**
I give notice that:	**John Sparrow**
is applying to the:	**Portside Borough Council**
for planning permission for:	**Erection of single storey dwelling and garage**

Any owner* of the land or tenant** who wishes to make representations about this application should write to the council at

Town Hall, Colonial Square, Portside

by **22 August 2009**

*'owner' means a person having a freehold interest or a leasehold interest the unexpired term of which is not less than seven years, or, in the case of development consisting of the winning or working of minerals, a person entitled to an interest in a mineral in the land (other than oil, gas, coal, gold or silver).

**'tenant' means a tenant of an agricultural holding any part of which is comprised in the land.

Signed

William Turnup

On behalf of
Date   1 August 2009

Statement of owners' rights
The grant of planning permission does not affect owners' right to retain or dispose of their property, unless there is some provision to the contrary in an agreement or in a lease.

Statement of agricultural tenants' rights
The grant of planning permission for non-agricultural development may affect agricultural tenants' security of tenure.

Figure 7.9

Notice of a planning application has to be sent to anyone who owns part of the application site

PLANNING APPLICATION FEES

TYPE OF APPLICATION	APPLICATION FEE
■ Full application for erection of all types of dwelling, inc flats	£335 for each dwelling
■ Outline application for the erection of all types of dwelling	£335 for each 0.1 hectare (rounded up)
■ Approval of reserved matters	£335 for each dwelling
■ Extension or alteration to existing dwellings	£150
■ Change of use of non-residential building to dwelling	£335 for each dwelling created
■ Sub-division of single dwelling to more than one dwelling	£335 for each additional dwelling created
■ Outbuilding in garden	£150
■ Varying or removing condition	£170
■ Renewal of planning permission	£170
■ Discharging conditions householder development	£25
other development	£85

EXEMPTION AND CONCESSIONS

■ Re-application for same type of development	
by same applicant, within 12 months of:	no fee
1 date of refusal of permission	
2 date of grant of permission	
3 date of submission of withdrawn application	
Limited to one application per property	
■ Application required because permitted development	no fee
rights removed by condition or article 4 direction	
■ Alternative schemes submitted simultaneously	highest fee plus half the remaining fees
■ Extension or alteration of a dwelling for access, safety,	
health or comfort of a disabled person	no fee

Figure 7.10

There is a fee to pay the council for making most planning applications which go up periodically and these are the fees applying to England as at October 2009

are set separately for each UK country by the respective government. The amount varies according to the project and there are exemptions and concessions.

Fees applicable to England are shown in Figure 7.10 (see above) but, since they go up periodically, do check the current level with the council. The rules on fees can be complicated so, if you're in any doubt, speak directly to the planning department to confirm the fee calculation for your application. If the council finds an application is technically invalid, the fee must be repaid to the applicant. Once planning permission is granted, an additional fee is payable to the council to approve any matters covered by conditions.

PLANS AND DRAWINGS

Every planning application must have a location plan, usually based on an Ordnance Survey map at a scale of 1:2,500 or 1:1,250 (see Figure 7.6 on pages 76–77). Councils have Ordnance Survey maps for their areas and can sell you photocopy extracts showing your site. Alternatively, there are websites selling Ordnance Survey maps and some large towns have a shop which acts as an Ordnance Survey agency. These maps though, are, expensive compared with council photocopies. Ordnance Survey maps can be out of date and whole estates and many individual properties are sometimes missed off, so check all surrounding buildings are shown. Your location plan needs

to identify the application site and show adjoining properties and roads. The application site must be outlined in red. Normally these are the property boundaries but it should include at least the site of all new building work and/or all areas in which a change of use will take place. If you own or control property outside the application site, outline this with a blue line. Felt pen is suitable for drawing red and blue lines on location plans. Write on the plan the address of the site, the date and the scale. The location plan (and all other scale application plans and drawings) is also supposed to include a scale bar to enable the scale to be checked as plans can be printed from electronically transmitted documents, or electronically scanned and re-printed.

With full planning applications you need to submit a site plan, also known as a block or site layout plan. This should usually be drawn to a scale of 1:500 and show such features as:

■ boundaries, existing and proposed;

■ buildings, existing and proposed;

■ buildings on adjoining land;

■ roads, pavements, verges and

CHAPTER SEVEN ● PREPARING THE PLANNING APPLICATION

footpaths;
■ existing and proposed access;
■ any work within public roads, pavements, etc;
■ parking areas;
■ trees and other natural features;
■ proposed landscaping;
■ existing and proposed drains, sewers, cesspools, septic tanks;
■ uses to be made of parts of the site not being built on.

Where your application is for full permission involving new buildings, you must have floor plans and elevations showing the front, back and side views of buildings. The sort of details these show are:
■ design and layout;
■ size and heights;
■ materials and finishes;
■ colour and texture of the exterior;
■ floor levels in relation to a fixed point off site;
■ changes in ground level;
■ construction of access;
■ position of all doors and windows;
■ extensions and alterations shaded to distinguish them from the existing building.

Some councils ask for additional plans, for example, roof plans and section drawings through the building. Where the project is an extension or a conversion, you'll need drawings of the building as it exists and as proposed, so the council can assess the changes and alterations you wish to make.

With outline planning applications, you can put in the same sort of drawings as you would for full applications but you don't have to. They only need illustrate what you have in mind, so they don't have to be precise or complete. For outline applications in England, you have to provide, at least, an indicative site layout including where the access would be. Mark all illustrative drawings clearly with such phrases as 'for illustrative purposes only', as their function is to help demonstrate that a site can take the sort of building you want. Unless you make it very clear that they're only for illustrative purposes, you might find them being assessed and judged as your final proposal.

The presentation of application drawings is very important – an attractive set of drawings can make the difference between success and failure of an application (some examples of drawings are given in Figures 7.11 and 7.12, see pages 86–89).

Think seriously about getting

PLANNING APPLICATION DRAWINGS FOR A NEW HOME

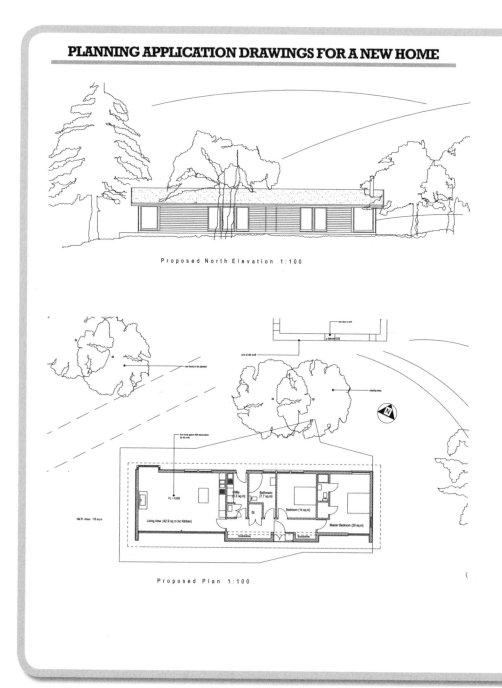

Proposed North Elevation 1:100

Proposed Plan 1:100

Planning application drawings for new homes show the site,

Proposed East Elevation 1:100

Figure 7.11

floor plans and elevations (courtesy of Constructive Individuals)

PLANNING APPLICATION
DRAWINGS FOR AN EXTENSION

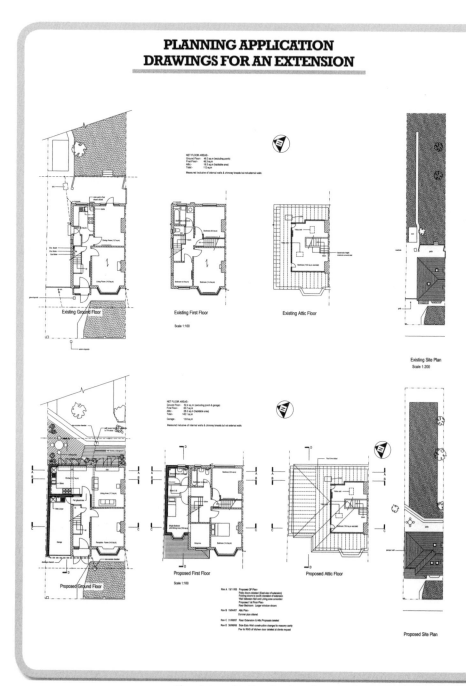

Planning application drawings for extensions show the building before

and after the proposed work (courtesy of Constructive Individuals)

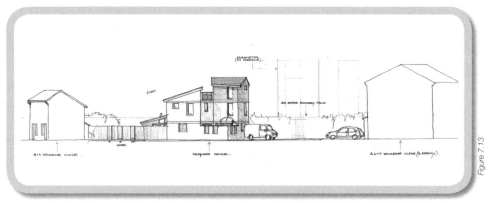

Figure 7.13

An artist's impression helps to show how the building will fit into its setting
(courtesy of Constructive Individuals)

them done professionally by someone who can show you previous work of a good standard. This doesn't mean you have to hand over the whole application to him or her; avoid using anyone who tells you otherwise. If you're buying a house from a self-build package company, it usually supplies floor plans and elevations for the house-type you want and you'll just have to get a site plan drawn, which shouldn't cost a great deal.

Many designers use computer aided design (CAD) to produce drawings. In the right hands this technology can create impressive looking drawings, but some CAD drawings can appear bland or stark. It's important for you to see the sort of drawings you'd be getting when you're deciding who to use. One advantage of CAD drawings is that they can be sent to the council electronically rather than having to supply a number of paper copies.

You're not confined to submitting only the drawings specified by the council and it's open to you to include any other illustrative material that might help portray your scheme. This could be an artist's impression showing the proposed building in its setting as it would be seen from principal viewpoints with adjoining buildings, trees, hedges and so on (see Figure 7.13 above). Sophisticated computer programmes allow the same thing to be done electronically with the building inserted into photographs of the vicinity, and even for moving images to be produced travelling around and through the planned building. If a three dimensional representation would help, perhaps where the structure is complicated or innovative, you can get a model made. Most applications don't need additional drawings and models, and they can be expensive, so don't get carried away. Once any illustrative material has been prepared, review it critically before sending it to the council to ensure is does actually present the project in the best light and doesn't, for example, over-emphasise its prominence or impact.

DESIGN AND ACCESS STATEMENTS

Certain applications in England and in Wales have to be accompanied by a design and access statement and, in Scotland, by a design statement. In England, extensions, alterations (outside AONBs and Conservation Areas) and changes of use, not involving physical works, don't require a statement but all others do, including new dwellings. In Scotland, only applications for new dwellings in Conservation Areas, National Scenic Areas and a few other specially designated areas, need a design statement. In Wales, new house applications and applications concerning Listed Buildings have to be accompanied by a design and access statement but extensions and alterations don't. The purpose is to provide information on design and/or access and show how they've been taken into account. Councils and the various governments publish guidance on content to which you should refer but the sort of issues to cover include:

■ context of the site;
■ relevant policies;
■ design principles;
■ proposed use;
■ amount of development;
■ layout;
■ scale;
■ landscaping;
■ appearance;
■ vehicle access and parking;
■ pedestrian and cycle access;
■ disabled access.

These statements were created with large-scale projects in mind and for small-scale residential proposals, statements are likely to be quite simple. Unless the site is in a sensitive location, many of the points can be covered in a sentence each and the whole statement might only comprise one or two sides of A4 paper (see Figure 7.14 (right)).

With outline applications many details won't be known and you might only be able to set out broad principles. In England, outline applications have to include information on use, number of units and minimum and maximum dimensions, and this information can be incorporated in your design and access statement. If you're not clear what's required in a statement, speak to a planning officer or enlist the help of a planning consultant to prepare the statement for you.

SPECIALISTS' REPORTS

Depending on the circumstances of your proposal and the area in which it's located, the council might require you to submit one or more specialists' reports with the application. Such reports can include access/highways, flood risk, trees, ecology/wildlife, drainage, contamination, energy performance, renewable energy or waste disposal. For applications in England you can get an idea of what might be sought by looking at the council's local

PLOT ADJOINING 32 CRANKSHAFT LANE, CHISEL POINT

Context
The site is in a mainly residential road with a variety of sizes and styles of houses, particularly on the eastern side of the road. There is a primary school adjoining to the south. Properties on the western side of Crankshaft Lane are mainly two-storey detached and semi-detached houses. Many houses are rendered with slate roofs, although there is brick, stone and some tile roofs.

Use
The proposed use is residential.

Amount
One three-bedroom house of 125 square metres.

Layout
The proposed house would be built on a similar building line to 32 and 34 Crankshaft Lane and the houses farther to the west. Garden space would be to the rear, where there would be a patio, and at the front. An existing access point would be used. Two parking spaces for the

list of requirements, otherwise your pre-application consultation with the council should indicate whether any reports are needed.

DESIGN & ACCESS STATEMENT

new house would be inside the front boundary. On the ground floor there would be a sitting room, dining room, kitchen, utility room and WC. On the first floor there would be a master bedroom with en suite shower room, two bedrooms and a bathroom.

Scale
The proposed two-storey house would be 7.0 m wide, 9.0 m deep (excluding porch) and 8.0 m high.

Landscaping
A new hedge would be planted along the front boundary with Crankshaft Lane. Three trees or shrubs would be planted on the new boundary between 32 Crankshaft Lane and the proposed house. The existing trees in the rear garden would be retained.

Appearance
The house would be rendered, with brick coins and decorative lintels, and a slate roof. The roof would be pitched, with the ridge running north/south, and a pitched roof over a rear-projecting gable. There would be a small porch in the west (front) elevation.

Vehicle access and parking
Access would be via the existing access point. Access and parking arrangements to 32 Crankshaft Lane would be unaffected. There would be a turning area in front of the property. Two parking spaces for the proposed dwelling would be located just inside the front boundary at the northern end.

Pedestrian and cycle access
Pedestrian and cycle access would be shared with the vehicle accesses. There is adequate garden space around the proposed houses for cycle storage.

Disabled access
The parking and turning area is level and would not present a problem for disabled people. It would be possible for a vehicle to pull up close to the front doors. The buildings would comply with Part M of the building regulations.

Conclusion
The proposed development represents an appropriate response to the nature of the site and surrounding area and provides the opportunity to improve the appearance of the land.

Figure 7.14

The necessity to submit some of this information can be a box-ticking exercise and, as long as something is said, the council will consider honour has been satisfied. It's, therefore, as well to discuss the necessary scope or level of detail before thinking about

SUPPORTING LETTER/PLANNING STATEMENT

29 January 2009

Head of Planning and Building Control
Pentup District Council, St Clod
Penalty CN15 5WQ

For the attention of Ainslie Gripp

Dear Sir

LEEWARD, PRIMARY PARK, MARZEL CN17 7BD
PLANNING APPLICATION — ERECTION OF TWO DWELLINGS

We enclose a planning application for two dwellings at this
site. The application is being submitted electronically and
includes: completed application form, relevant ownership and
agricultural certificates, design and access statement, cheque
payable to Pentup District Council for £670.00 (by post),
application drawings 166 P01, P02 A & P03C and tree report.

Background
This application is made after the refusal of previous
applications 05/0931/F and 07/0237/F, which was then turned down
at appeal. These proposals were for building on a different part
of the site. We reconsidered the potential of the site in light
of those decisions and the current proposal was drawn up in
consultation with your planning officer. The design is described
in the design and access statement prepared by our architects
and has been agreed with the planning officer.

Proposal
The proposal is to build a pair of semi-detached houses to
the west of the existing three-bedroom bungalow, Leeward. The
existing access points would be utilised. Leeward would be
unaffected, other than the consequent changes to its garden.

Planning policy
Structure Plan policy S1 says development should be compatible
with the conservation and enhancement of the county's character
and distinctiveness. Policy S2 states development must respect
local character and relate positively to townscape character.
   Local plan policy DN1 requires development to be integrated
with surroundings. Policy DN2 says that proposals should respect
traditional patterns of development and materials and make

You can justify and explain your proposal in a covering letter/

provision for cycle parking, waste storage and disabled access. Policy HO5 states that infill housing will be permitted within Marzel. Policy HO21 requires the effective use of land and dwelling types to be appropriate to the mix of households in the area.

Assessment

The principle of the proposal is established in local plan policy HO5.

The design of the building reflects the style, proportions, materials and features of the area. The siting would be consistent with the pattern of development on this side of the road. It would relate well to the neighbouring houses and preserve the setting of the conservation area. The proposal would also provide the opportunity to enhance the site as a whole and so the setting of the conservation area opposite.

The houses would have a good amount of amenity space around them, providing ample scope for waste storage, cycle parking and disabled parking. The front of the site, in front of the proposed houses, has a gentle slope and would provide relatively easy disabled access.

The area has a mix of housing types and two four-bedroom houses would be appropriate to the area. The proposals would make an effective use of land to provide additional housing.

The planning officers have indicated in pre-application discussions acceptance of the principle of the development, the size of the building and the detailed design, to which they helpfully contributed.

Conclusion

The proposed development represents an appropriate form of development to the site and setting, consistent with development plan policy.

If you have any questions about the application, please contact us.

Yours faithfully

Nigel and Wendy Hope

Figure 7.15

planning statement, referring to relevant planning policies

instructing a specialist. Discuss the council's requirements with any professional you're using as your planning consultant or designer might be able to provide some of the information. If a full report is necessary, you'll need a specialist so ask your planning consultant for recommendations, contact relevant professional bodies or look in Yellow Pages/Yell.com. For most small-scale residential developments, single houses and extensions you won't have to commission a specialist report but, where you do, it will obviously increase your costs and, since they can take a while to produce, commission the professional(s) as early as possible.

FINANCIAL CONTRIBUTIONS

When granting planning permission for new houses or flats, many councils demand the payment of money which they put towards infrastructure needed in connection with new development. Examples include contributions towards public transport, school places, play grounds or leisure facilities. In practice it's a local tax on development. Usually, this means you'll have sign a legal planning agreement (see Chapter

1) committing to pay the sum of money when the work starts or before the building is occupied. Some councils expect a signed document to be submitted with the application and some provide standard formats for you to use. Others draw up a document once the application is submitted. Many councils also insist on payment of their costs for preparing or considering the planning agreement. As with any legal document, it's advisable to get your solicitor to draw up or check it before you sign. If permission is refused or the development doesn't go ahead for some reason, you aren't obliged to pay the contributions but you might still be left with your solicitor's bill.

SUPPORTING LETTER/ PLANNING STATEMENT

Beyond a design and access statement and specialists' reports, councils often include a separate planning statement as one of their requirements to accompany a planning application. In the case of simple projects, the application forms and drawings might give adequate information for the council to be able to assess your project. If you're making an outline

LETTER WRITING TIPS

DO

■ make your points as brief and concise as possible

■ adopt a clear, calm and objective style

■ deal only with planning matters – design, relationship with other buildings, previous planning permissions (see Part One)

■ draw attention to any similar planning permissions you know about

■ point out all positive physical factors – existing screening, seclusion of site, lack of overlooking windows in adjoining properties

■ describe any constraints that have dictated design or siting

■ refer to relevant planning policies and supplementary guidance and explain how your proposal complies with it

■ offer to meet the planning officer to discuss matters if he or she has questions or concerns

■ type the letter if possible – failing that, write very clearly

DON'T

■ just repeat what is said in the application form or design and access statement

■ tell the council that it can't refuse your application

■ point out examples of poor planning decisions in an attempt to justify your own application

■ catalogue your meetings with the planning officer where they went badly or describe exactly who said what and when

■ criticise the council or planning officers' behaviour

■ set out all your personal circumstances, unless there's a special reason why they're relevant and compelling

■ describe the proposal in great detail

■ mention plans for future development

application in England, you might need to set out the necessary information on use, number of units and minimum and maximum dimensions in a covering letter, if it's not going to be included elsewhere. Otherwise, even when it's not mandatory, it's usually worth writing a supporting letter/ statement whose purpose is to explain, justify and give more information about what you propose (see Figure 7.15 on page 94-95). There's no set format but headings might typically include:

■ description of the site;

■ any relevant background to the proposal;

■ planning history;

■ nature of the proposal;

■ relevant planning policy/ guidance;

■ any similar examples;

■ assessment in relation to planning policy.

Remember your application is going to be judged on the criteria in Chapter 4, and planning policy in particular, so focus on those issues. You don't need to go to great length under each heading. In the panel (on previous page) are some general suggestions for writing supporting letters.

Your letter needs to be as positive about the proposal as possible but making claims unsupportable on the facts of the case is counter-productive, as planning officers will check what you say for themselves. It's better to say too little than too much, because what you add as background information could be used against you in ways you can't always predict. Planning policy is complex and your scheme is important to you so if you have any doubts, leave the statement to your planning consultant or designer.

SUBMITTING THE APPLICATION

To recap, so far you should have:

■ filled in an application form ready to be copied or to be submitted on-line;

■ checked the application fee and written a cheque;

■ completed an ownership certificate and, if appropriate, completed a notice ready to send to the owner or tenant;

■ prepared a location plan and other drawings;

■ produced a design and access statement, if necessary;

■ obtained any specialists' reports required;

■ completed a legal agreement or draft, where a financial contribution is sought;

■ written a supporting letter/ planning statement, if appropriate.

If you're submitting paper copies of the documents, the application guidance notes will tell you how many copies of the planning application and supporting documents to submit – four or five sets of forms and drawings is usual, but check with the planning department if you're not sure. Only one copy of the ownership certificate needs to be included, if that's a separate document. Get the correct number of copies taken, making sure you keep at least one copy of the complete application for yourself. Remember to outline the site in red and other land in blue on each separate copy of the location plan. If you're sending a covering letter/statement, include a copy with each set of forms and drawings. You can submit just one letter but it's better that as many people as possible read your case in support, and consultees won't see the letter if you don't attach a copy to each application. Make all the copies up into sets and fix the papers together, putting the covering letter on top, and attach your cheque and ownership certificate to the first copy of the application. Check that you have the correct address for the district council's planning department and then post your application, or deliver it to the planning department personally.

If you're making the application on-line via the internet, the submission is somewhat simpler, once you have all the documents completed in electronic form. Ask any building designer or consultants you use to supply their drawings and documents in electronic file formats you're able to open on your computer. Check the location plan includes the red and blue lines. The

Planning Portal or council website gives instructions and checks you've completed all the required information. If not all the application documents are in electronic form, you do have the option to post the required number of copies of those to the council and you'll need to post the application fee cheque, unless your council accepts online payment.

applications

2

CHAPTER 8

THE PLANNING APPLICATION

Once your planning application is sent to the council, you don't have to take any further action and can wait for the decision. There are steps you can take, however, that will give your application the best chance of success. Figure 5.2 on page 44 demonstrates how councils deal with planning applications. This could be a good point at which to refresh your memory about the procedure.

REGISTRATION AND ACKNOWLEDGEMENT

The council first checks that your application is technically correct. This should be done within a few days of submission but the speed of councils' administration varies. You could find that a couple of weeks go by before the council writes telling you the application needs to be altered or asking for more information, and meanwhile your application won't have even begun to be assessed. When the application is validated and

ACKNOWLEDGEMENT LETTER

WYDMOOR DISTRICT COUNCIL

Mrs J Finess
The Larches
Holly Close
Beckfield YT8 9OK

My ref: 09/00897/FUL
Please ask for: Alfonse Damper
Telephone: 01878 750987
Date: 03 April 2009

Dear Sir/Madam

TOWN AND COUNTRY PLANNING ACT 1990

LOCATION: The Larches Holly Close YT8 9OK
PROPOSAL: Single storey rear extension
APPLICATION NO: 09/00897/FUL
DRAWING No(s):   SITE PLAN; PL2; PL3; PL4;
DATE RECEIVED: 1st April 2009

Thank you for your application, the details of which are shown above
and the fee of £150. Please quote the application number in all
enquiries. Please check the description and let me know immediately if
you feel it does not accurately describe your proposal.

The plans and documents you have submitted have not yet been fully
examined. If I find that your application is invalid because it does
not comply with the statutory requirements then I shall write to you
again as soon as I can.

The person dealing with your application is Alfonse Damper. If you
wish to discuss your application please ring during normal working
hours on 01878 750987.

If by 29th May 2009 you have not been given a decision you are
advised to contact this office for information about the progress of
your application. If after that date you are not satisfied with the
progress you can appeal to the Secretary of State for the Department
of Communities and Local Government against the local planning
authority's failure to issue a decision. You should appeal within six
months and you must use a form which is obtainable from The Planning
Inspectorate, Temple Quay House. 2 The Square, Temple Quay, Bristol
BSI 6PN. Alternatively you can lodge an appeal via the Internet by
going to www.planningportaI.gov.uk/pcs. A leaflet about this (DCS2) is
available from the Council on request.

Yours faithfully

Denzil Bosse

Development Manager

Figure 8.1

Having checked the application the council sends out an acknowledgement letter

registered, the council will write to you to acknowledge receipt (see Figure 8.1). To check whether your application has been accepted and is proceeding, get in touch with the planning department's administrative section a week after you sent the application and ask whether it's all right. Alternatively, if your council publishes applications on its website, check its status there. The acknowledgement letter sets out:

■ application reference number;
■ address of the property;
■ description of the development;
■ name of the planning officer dealing with the application (often called the 'case officer');
■ date the application was 'received' and validated by the council (the day after it arrives technically complete at the council offices);
■ date by which a decision should be made (eight weeks from validation);
■ rights to appeal, if a decision isn't made within eight weeks.

The letter can contain other information, such as the programme of planning committee meetings. Check that the information is correct, especially the description of development,

and, if you have questions about anything in the letter, contact the planning officer. Note the planning application reference number and quote it in any communication with the council. Sending an acknowledgement letter doesn't actually guarantee the application is technically correct and points can still be brought up later.

PUBLICITY AND CONSULTATION

When your application has been registered, the council carries out publicity. In most cases, this involves writing to neighbours telling them about the application. The letter tells them where to see the application, how to make comments and gives a period for making comments (21 days from when the letter was sent). Although comments are supposed to be made within this period, councils should take into account all letters and emails received before a decision is taken, and if the council is slow in sending out the letters, the application can be delayed. Many councils also publish a list of all planning applications in a local paper and on their websites each week and comments can be made by anyone, not just by the people who are notified directly. If you can persuade your neighbours to write to the council in support of your proposal or, at least, not to object, this will help to get your planning permission through. Certain types of application must be publicised by an official site notice which is put up by the council but this isn't needed for most residential applications. Some councils operate a voluntary site notice scheme, sending out a notice, usually printed on garish coloured card, at the same time as the acknowledgement letter, which you're asked to put up on the site where it can be seen by passers-by. Such schemes are entirely voluntary – despite what some councils imply – and you shouldn't be penalised because you don't display the notice, so the decision is yours. The disadvantage is that potential objectors could be alerted to your proposal who wouldn't otherwise know about it.

The planning department consults other council departments and outside bodies about applications. The parish council, highway authority and drainage authority are normally consulted about new houses. You can attend and often speak at parish council meetings when your application is considered and this can be worthwhile to explain or answer questions about your proposal. If you think you might want to take advantage of this opportunity, find out in advance when and where meetings are held as they can take place quite soon after an application is submitted. There are many other organisations who could be consulted, depending on the type of application and where the site is located, and this exercise is carried out at the same time as your application is publicised. You might have found out about consultees in your pre-application discussions but, if not, you can ask the planning officer who is being consulted. You can contact those bodies to check all is well but it's not usually necessary.

CONTACTING THE PLANNING OFFICER

Many council's websites enable you to monitor the progress of your application and see what consultees and members of the public are saying about it. Even where that's the case, it won't tell you the planning officer's view of your proposal until his final report is written. It's up to you to take the initiative and contact the officer, if you want to find out how your application is really doing. Occasionally officers will write or phone if there are changes they'd like to see made to an application but, otherwise, you'll probably not be contacted. Don't assume that because pre-application meetings went very well, your application will sail through, as new points can come up and officers can take a different view once your application is made. The planning officer is under no obligation to let you know about problems that come to light while the application is being assessed or that he's changed his mind. You can try contacting the planning officer a week or two after the application is registered to get any initial reaction, although he won't look very closely at an application until about a month after submission, by which time any objections and responses to consultation should have been made. At this early stage you can just check the officer has all the information he needs and is clear about the proposal and find out when to call back. The planning officer will come out to inspect the site at some point – normally turning up

unannounced – and it's not until after the inspection, and until comments are received, that he can tell you how the application is going. Unless you have a particular concern, leave it about a month from making your application to phone or email. When you speak to the planning officer, ask about:

■ any potential problems identified by planning officers or consultees;

■ objections received;

■ how any problems can be overcome and whether to amend the application;

■ any further information you can provide that would be helpful;

■ whether the decision is to be taken by the officers or by the committee;

■ which committee the application should go to, or when the delegated decision is likely to be taken;

■ when the officer has to write his report to committee by.

Hopefully, there'll be no difficulties with the application at this stage. In any event, it's wise to make at least one more phone call nearer the time of the decision to double-check nothing new has come up.

If applicable, make sure you have a chance to see the officer's report to committee, when it's published a week before the committee meeting.

OVERCOMING OBJECTIONS

Councils are very focussed on their target times for reaching decisions and, generally, won't delay a decision in order to allow amendments to be made or further information submitted. Some councils don't even allow further information to be submitted, unless they specifically request it. Consequently, there's often limited scope, if any, to overcome objections once an application has been submitted. Not all problems the officer might mention can be resolved through negotiation. For example, if the officer says your application conflicts fundamentally with council planning policy, probably nothing you can do will change his mind. Even when an officer feels an objection can't be overcome, he should still advise you how to make the application as acceptable as possible but this doesn't necessarily mean it will get his support. Discuss with the planning officer how best to deal with points raised. This could involve getting your drawings revised to

show changes in design, siting or layout, contacting a consultee, such as the highway authority, to talk about its requirements or altering a boundary position or window position to overcome a neighbour's concern. Letters of objection might be put straight on the application file or on the council's website, or can be kept confidential until a delegated decision is taken or the officer's report is published before the committee meeting. Even in the latter cases, the planning officer is allowed to tell you the substance of objections. Try speaking to neighbours or local people who object, if you think it will help, as it's obviously better not to have outstanding objections. If you reach an amicable solution, ask the objectors to write to the council withdrawing their objection. Avoid arguing with objectors, and try concentrating on the official channels if you don't get anywhere with them.

The council can put conditions on planning permission, where this is necessary to overcome problems that might otherwise cause the application to be refused. You have no say over whether the council imposes conditions (although you can appeal against them later) but sometimes applicants are asked if they'll 'agree' to a condition. Technically, this is meaningless, but you can, if you want, say what restrictions you could live with. An alternative to conditions is a planning obligation/agreement, which has wider scope than planning conditions (see Chapter 1) and can be a useful device to get around difficulties with applications. This should never be entered without proper professional advice, however.

Listen carefully to what the planning officer tells you and don't dismiss it lightly, although you don't have to amend your application if you don't agree with the changes suggested. This doesn't necessarily mean that your application will be refused but it's less likely to succeed and you have to weigh this up – you could let the application run and, if refused, re-apply, or you could appeal if the council refuses permission. This might be the moment to think about getting advice from a planning consultant because, unless you're familiar with planning, you might not be able to judge when the planning officer is pushing his luck, the significance of the objections or your chances of success.

If you're going to try to overcome objections, make sure the planning officer knows. Where you supply new material, the council might re-publicise and re-consult and a further period is given for comment, during which time the council won't issue a decision.

PLANNING OFFICER'S REPORT

Where your application is to be decided by planning officers (delegated decision), the decision is taken at some time after the publicity and consultation period ends. The officer dealing with the application writes a report – often referred to as a 'delegated report' – and passes it to a more senior officer for checking and the decision is made. In Northern Ireland all decisions on planning applications are made in this way by officers of the Planning Service. There's normally little scope to react to an officer's delegated report before the decision is taken.

A minority of applications go to a planning committee meeting and the planning officer writes a report on the application, concluding with a recommendation, which is included on an agenda for a committee meeting (an example of such a report is given in Figure 8.2 on pages 108-109). The officer can usually give you a good idea quite early on which meeting your application should get to. The target date for all decisions on applications of less than 10 dwellings is eight weeks from submission – councils aim for this with widely varying degrees of success – and a committee date for your application isn't definite until the agenda is settled. Committee agendas must be available for the public to see five clear days before the meeting (three days in Wales) and you can look on the council's website or go to the planning department to get a copy or read the officer's report on your application, but sometimes councils can be persuaded to email, fax or post a copy.

Officers' reports vary in length and quality – some are a few, inadequate paragraphs which tell councillors and you virtually nothing, while others are thorough and run to several sides of paper. The language used can be so obscure such that you scarcely recognise the property you have lived in for years. Obviously, a recommendation for approval of planning permission is good but might not mean you can relax entirely – if there's local opposition to your application, objectors could be working on councillors.

If the recommendation is for refusal, find out what reasons led to this conclusion and check the accuracy of facts, such as heights of buildings, distances to boundaries and nature of the use. If the report contains factual mistakes, speak to the planning officer straight away, saying what you think is incorrect and ask what the officer can do about it. Follow this up with a letter recording the errors made and asking for these to be pointed out to councillors at the committee meeting. You'll, no doubt, disagree with statements of opinion in the report, which could be the officer's views on the appearance of buildings, effect on the character of the area, or the size of buildings. You can do little about statements of opinion, as they won't be changed just because you dispute them, no matter how unjustified they seem to you.

LOBBYING COUNCILLORS

You can contact councillors to

PLANNING OFFICER'S REPORT

Application number: AN/09/0245
Address: Land at 52 East Drive, Bucklegate
Proposal: Outline erection of detached house and garage
Applicant: Mr & Mrs P Merritt
Case officer: Geraldine Knutson

Consultations
5 letters of objection — over-development, loss of trees, loss of privacy, dangerous access, garden grabbing
Town council — objects on grounds of increased traffic on already busy road and over-large building
Bucklegate Conservation Group — objects on grounds of over-development, out of keeping with attractive low density residential area and protected trees at risk
Highway authority — removal of frontage hedge required to give adequate visibility to north, recommends conditions

Development Plan Policies
Borough Plan policies: H2, 113, and ENV7
Structure Plan: SE1, SE2 and D7

Site description
The site lies within the developed area of Bucklegate in an area of spacious detached housing. The application site extends to 0.04 hectares of level grassland. It is bounded by established hedgerows on the east and west boundaries and close board fence on the north and south. There is a group of three protected oak trees in the south-east corner.

Relevant planning history
AN/07/0658 — erection of pair of semi-detached houses refused 28/10/07

Proposal
The application is made in outline with all matters reserved. The dwelling would be two-storey 6.0 m—6.5 m in width, 7.0 m—7.5 m deep and 7.0 m—7.5 m high. The illustrative site layout shows the dwelling to be sited 5.0 m from the front boundary with a single garage close to the northern boundary.

The planning officer's report describes the proposal and sets out all the considerations

Main issues
Whether the dwelling would be in keeping with surrounding development and adversely affect protected trees.

Assessment
Housing development is acceptable in principle in this area. However, it is considered that development of this small site would be cramped and out of character in this low density area. The development, if permitted, would have an incongruous and uncomfortable relationship to the existing pattern of development, contrary to Borough Plan policy H2. Although only in outline, concern is expressed over the likely proximity of the rear of the house to the protected trees. If permitted the location of the dwelling could give rise to an application to fell the trees that would be difficult to resist. Due to the access requirements to serve the development, the frontage hedge would be lost to meet the visibility standards of the Borough Engineer. This proposal has met with unanimous objection from local people and is considered unacceptable.

Recommendation
Refusal

Reasons
1 Over development contrary to Borough Plan policy H2 and Structure Plan policy SE2
2 Adverse effect on landscape contrary to Borough Plan policy ENV7
3 Unneighbourly, poor relationship to existing development, Borough Plan policy H3 and Structure Plan policy SE1 and D7

Figure 8.2

and ends with a recommendation on whether planning permission should be given

LETTER TO A COUNCILLOR

Councillor Isfahan
28 West Street Terrace
Potherwick
PW32 1JP

21st February 2009

Dear Councillor Isfahan

PLANNING APPLICATION FOR A DWELLING TO THE REAR OF BIRDCAGE HOUSE,
HOLBROOK STREET
(REF: 09/PO/213)

I refer to our telephone conversation and, as suggested, write to
confirm the points we discussed. The planning application is going to
this Thursday's planning committee meeting and the planning officer has
decided to recommend refusal of the application in his report.

The only objections concern the effect on one neighbouring property
and design. The neighbouring property is 15 metres away and has only
two windows facing my proposed house: a dining room and an upstairs
bathroom. There is already a hedge and shrubs in front of the dining
room window and this can be supplemented with new planting. In any
event, the main aspect of the neighbouring property is southwards,
away from my plot.

The planning officer has commented that the proposed render and
feature board finish above ground floor level is not appropriate in this
location and I am willing to change this to the planning officer's
preferred finish, stock bricks, as proposed for the ground floor.

How little the neighbouring property would be affected can best be
appreciated by looking on site and I believe committee members would
find it helpful to see the site for themselves before making the
decision. I would be grateful, therefore, if the decision could be
deferred on Thursday to allow a committee site visit to take place.

Yours sincerely

Hubert Berry

Mr H P Berry

Figure 8.3

You can write to councillors pointing out the advantages and acceptability of your scheme when the application is going to be decided by the planning committee discuss your application at any stage in the process – subject to the council's rules on this – and we looked earlier at the merits of speaking to councillors before making an application (see Chapter 6). If you discover that the planning officer is going to recommend your application for refusal, think about contacting councillors but, remember, some councils do discourage lobbying, and so the members of such authorities won't be receptive to your approach. If your application looks likely to be refused by the officers in a delegated decision, you can ask a councillor to request it goes to committee for a decision instead. There are often quite early deadlines for such councillor requests. Unless you know one personally, find out the names of district councillors who are on the committee which will decide your application, as some councils have more than one planning committee. The planning department can give you their names and addresses. You can make contact in several ways but do act quickly if the officer's report has been published as you'll have only a matter of days before the committee meeting.

If you decide to phone one or two local councillors do it at a time likely to be most convenient for them, because if you catch them at an inconvenient moment your task is that much harder. Some councillors hold regular surgeries and, if time permits, go along and meet the councillors there. Otherwise, tell them about the application and why you disagree with the planning officer's assessment. Councillors are more sympathetic to personal circumstances than planning officers, even though personal matters aren't supposed to be taken into account. Councillors probably won't have seen your application or looked at the site, so invite them around to see both the property and your proposal. You can write a letter to some or all of the committee members, but this can be less effective than phoning and meeting them. Such a letter should be brief and to the point to maximise the chances of it being read and the points taken on board (see the example in Figure 8.3 opposite). In the letter, request that the committee makes a site visit, as they're more likely to overrule an officer's recommendation if they've seen the property for themselves. A committee site visit would delay a decision until the next committee meeting so they might not agree in order not to go over the decision target date. When approaching councillors, don't criticise planning officers or the council but explain and give the selling points of your scheme and ask for their advice. If you disagree with them, don't argue because, frustrating as it might be, they hold the power over your application. Good councillors will put your points of view to the committee, even if they don't share them entirely. Ask what the councillors are prepared to do to help you.

WITHDRAWING APPLICATIONS

You can withdraw your planning application at any time before a decision is taken, although the advantages of this are limited. Withdrawing an application means that a refusal won't be entered on the planning record of the property but, the fact that a withdrawal is shown on the record, usually suggests an application was going down anyway. You can't appeal if you withdraw. Getting a refusal doesn't stop you making a new application and the council will keep the file on a withdrawn application and refer to it if another application is made. If the application is going to committee and you lobby councillors, there's some chance the application will be approved or at least not refused outright. If you decide to withdraw your application, you'll need to do it in writing.

PLANNING COMMITTEE MEETINGS

Planning committee meetings are open to the public and most councils allow members of the public to speak at meetings. At the remainder, you're not allowed to speak and you can only sit and listen. The sort of large-scale and controversial applications that typically go to committee are discussed in turn by councillors. The committee works through the officers' reports in the agenda. Each application is introduced by the chairman which is followed by a presentation by planning officers, describing the proposal, providing any new last minute information and outlining the main issues. The councillors then have their opportunity to say their piece after which there's a vote.

Find out whether your council allows public speaking at committee meetings and what the rules and arrangements are as this varies but the council should let you know well in advance, if it has such a policy. This usually involves registering your intention to speak and the deadline for doing that can be anything from a few days beforehand to a few minutes before the meeting is due to start. Where the recommendation is for refusal or there have been objections, go along to speak up for your proposal and counter what objectors say. If the recommendation is for approval and you're sure there won't be any objectors speaking, it might not be necessary to speak. Normally you'll only have two or three minutes to make your points so concentrate on answering any objections and on the advantages of the scheme. Councillors are lay people not planning experts (you might be shocked by what can be a low-level of debate at committee meetings) and strength of feeling is often more influential than technicalities. Having registered to speak, a council official will explain the mechanics and how the speeches are timed and the

chairman will call you up when the time comes.

If you do decide to go to the committee, check the date, time and place of the meeting. Some councils operate a system where the applications that people come to hear are dealt with first, but otherwise it's a question of waiting for your application to come up. The planning officer should be able to give you an idea before the meeting of when the committee is likely to reach yours. Have pen and paper with you ready to take notes of what's said, as this could be useful later – although it's often difficult to follow committee procedure, or sometimes even to hear who's saying what. Councillors don't have to follow the planning officer's recommendation but they usually do and recommendations aren't overturned without some debate. If your application is considered to be clear-cut – one way or the other – it probably won't be discussed to any great extent and it will move quickly to a vote. If you can't attend, you can find out the decision by telephoning the planning department later in the day or the next day, depending on the time of the meeting. One of four decisions is possible: refusal; delegated; deferred; or permission.

REFUSAL OF PLANNING PERMISSION

A refused planning permission isn't necessarily the end of your project. A decision notice is sent to you a week or so after the planning officer's delegated decision has been taken or the committee meeting has been held. It gives the reasons why the council says it refuses permission (see the example in Figure 8.4 opposite). Read these carefully, especially where the officer recommended approval. The number of reasons given doesn't always reflect how defective the council considered your application to be – one soundly based reason is harder to overcome than half a dozen spurious ones and many councils do go for quantity rather than quality. It's quite possible that you won't understand all the reasons as they're usually written in technical language, so ask the planning officer to explain them.

DELEGATED DECISION

For technical reasons, a decision can't always be formally made at a committee meeting. Instead the decision is taken in principle and the final issuing of the decision is delegated to the most senior planning officer, who does this once the outstanding matter is resolved. Councils are keen to meet their target time for making decisions, so are usually reluctant to delegate decisions where this would result in missing the target date. Delegation can happen where:

■ a consultation period hasn't expired at the date of the meeting;

■ further information, not likely to change the decision, has yet to be provided (eg details of drainage arrangements);

■ the council wants small revisions to be made to the application and asks for amended drawings to be submitted which will then be approved;

■ a planning obligation/agreement, either required by the council or offered by the applicant, is to be drawn up.

DEFERRED DECISION

Decisions are deferred in the same sorts of circumstances as they're delegated, except the committee wants to make the final decision itself, usually because it's still uncertain whether permission will

DECISION NOTICE REFUSING PLANNING PERMISSION

HARCOURT DISTRICT COUNCIL

Application Number: DC/09/1792

TOWN AND COUNTRY PLANNING ACT, 1990
TOWN AND COUNTRY PLANNING (GENERAL DEVELOPMENT PROCEDURE) ORDER

On behalf of: Sidney Bridger

In pursuance of their powers under the above-mentioned Act and Order, the Council hereby REFUSE to permit the works specified hereunder, that is to say:

Demolition of existing extension and erection of single-storey and two-storey extension (Full Planning)

Site at Bottle Street Harcourt

as shown on Plan and Application Number DC/09/1792 submitted to the Council on 31/07/2009. The reasons for the Council's decision to refuse to permit the above works are specified hereunder.

1 The extensions by reason of their overall size and design fail to reflect the scale and character of the existing dwelling contrary in particular to Policy D8, D12 and D27 of the Harcourt District Local Development Framework: General Development Control Policies (2008) and CI4 of the Harcourt District Local Development Framework: Core Strategy (2008).
2 The proposed two-storey and single storey extensions by virtue of their design, form and scale would not relate sympathetically to the existing dwelling contrary to policy DC12 of the Harcourt District Local Development Framework: General Development Control Policies (2008).

This decision is based on the following submitted plans/documents:
Location and Block plan Drwg no. 09-11-200 Received 31st July 09
Existing Floor plan and Elevations Drwg no. 09-11-11 Received 31st July 09
Proposed Floor and Elevations Drwg no. 09-11-10B Received 31st July 09
Design and Access Statement Received 31st July 09
Supporting Planning Statement Received 31st July 09

J Meeley

HEAD OF DEVELOPMENT   Date: 10/09/2009

Figure 8.4

A notice refusing permission gives the reasons why the council says permission was turned down

be granted. Again, target-date pressure makes councils reluctant to defer decisions. A main reason why applications are often deferred is to give the committee the opportunity to inspect the site. A deferred application will be put on the agenda for a future committee meeting and, if you attend the committee meeting, it should be clear why an application is either delegated or deferred. Otherwise, contact the planning officer to find out what you need to do. A deferred decision also provides an opportunity for lobbying or over coming objections.

PLANNING PERMISSION

The grant of permission gives you the right to carry out your development but remember there are other consents you might need (see Chapter 1). Applications for some of these (such as Listed Building or Conservation Area Consent) are normally made and decided by the council at the same time as planning permission, and the planning officer should tell you whether you need other consents at an initial meeting, or when your planning application is submitted. The decision notice is sent to you (see example in Figure

8.5 on page 118-119), sometimes with a copy of the application stamped by the council. Put this away in a safe place and use a spare copy of the decision notice and application if you need a working copy to draw on or to give to builders and others. The permission will be subject to conditions, even if it's just the standard time limit for beginning work, but there are likely to be others. Read these carefully and the reasons given for them. Conditions are written in semi-legal language and are frequently badly worded. You might get your planning permission but the conditions could make it worthless to you, for example, if you intend building a two-storey house but a condition limits your outline permission to a single-storey building. It's important that you understand the implications of conditions before you act on a planning permission. If you've any doubts, go through each condition with the planning officer to find out exactly what they restrict or what additional information is required. If you're not satisfied by what the officer says or are still unsure about the conditions, take advice from a planning consultant.

DISCHARGING CONDITIONS

It's common to find conditions that require you to seek further approval from the council for some aspect of your scheme, typically the details of external building materials and finishes to be used. This involves submitting the details the council wants, together with a fee. Many councils provide forms for discharging conditions, as the process is known, but forms aren't compulsory. You must though state the property address and application reference, and which condition you're seeking to discharge. If you have to take samples of materials to the council, mark each one clearly with a label giving the application reference, property name and condition number. Where there are several conditions to discharge, try to submit all the details together, otherwise you'll pay a fee for each separate conditions application.

FURTHER ACTION

Where you've obtained outline permission, assuming you want to go ahead, you need to get the council's approval of the details – the reserved matters – which involves getting a site plan, floor plans and elevations drawings

(see Chapter 7). You've three years in which to make that application. When you have either the reserved matters approved or a full permission, check whether you need building regulations consent – the council's building control section should be able to tell you about this. Check what time limit is set out in the conditions for beginning work on your approved development and keep it in mind, if you don't intend to start work in the immediate future. Make certain you renew an unimplemented permission before it expires, or start building within the time limit, having first discharged all the conditions that require further approvals before work commences, to keep the permission alive. The sort of work that constitutes beginning development includes demolition, construction work, digging foundation trenches, laying pipes or mains and laying out or building a road. Photograph and get documentary proof of such work and ask the council to confirm in writing that the permission has been validly implemented.

If permission is refused, you've three courses of action: accept the decision; make another planning application; and/or appeal against the decision. Which you

DECISION NOTICE GRANTING
PLANNING PERMISSION

ROSEBUND BOROUGH COUNCIL

TOWN AND COUNTRY PLANNING ACT 1990
Town and Country Planning (General Development Procedure)
Order 1995

PLANNING PERMISSION
Applicant: Mr D & Mrs K Nibbles
Agent: Spare Dude Planning Consultants

LOCATION: 3 Button Drive Stick MC14 5OP
PROPOSAL: Single storey rear extension & extension of
pitched roof
APPLICATION NO: 09/00957/FUL
DATE RECEIVED: 29th April 2009
DRAWING NO(s): SITE PLAN; SK/PL3; SK/PL7; SK/PL8; SK/PL9;

The Council has given consideration to the application
and plans as specified above, and hereby gives notice of
its decision to GRANT PLANNING PERMISSION subject to the
following conditions: -

1 The development hereby permitted shall be begun before the
  expiration of three years from the date of this permission.
2 The development hereby permitted shall not be carried out
  other than in complete accordance with the approved plans
  and specifications or as otherwise may be agreed in writing
  by the local planning authority.
3 The external surfaces of the extension hereby approved
  shall be constructed of materials to match those of the
  existing building. Where the new materials differ from
  those of the existing building, details (and samples if
  requested by the local planning authority) of those new
  materials shall be submitted to and approved by the local
  planning authority in writing before any part of the
  development is begun.

A decision notice granting planning permission sets

Reasons:
1 In order to comply with Section 91(1) of the Town and Country Planning Act 1990 as amended by Section 51 of the Planning and Compulsory Purchase Act 2004.
2 In order to achieve satisfactory development of the site.
3 To ensure the proposed development is visually satisfactory and does not prejudice the appearance of the locality.

The Development Plan policies taken into account in deciding this application are listed below. The full text of the policies may be inspected at the Council's offices.
DC4   Development in the Metropolitan Green Belt
DC34   Achieving High Quality Development
DC48   Extensions to Dwellings

Reason(s) for this decision
1 The proposal demonstrates reasonable compliance with the relevant policies of the Development Plan and there are no other material considerations.

Date: 6 June 2009

Signed: *D Squibb*

Daphne Squibb, Director of Sustainable Communities

IMPORTANT — YOUR ATTENTION IS DRAWN TO THE NOTES ATTACHED

Figure 8.5

out conditions and brief reasons for giving permission

do depends on how important the project is and why permission was refused. See whether the reasons for refusal relate to points of detail, such as design or not complying with council standards, or whether they relate to principle, for example, the development is in the wrong place or conflicts directly with planning policies. Points of detail can usually be overcome by amending the scheme so making a revised application is then probably the quickest and simplest way to get permission. The officer's report should give a good idea of what changes the council would want to see. Go back through the steps described in this Part, starting with discussing the application with the planning officer and think again about professional help. You don't pay a fee to the council for one revised application made within a year of a refusal. A refusal on principle is harder to deal with and a new application, even with revisions, is unlikely to be approved by the council but you could try talking to councillors. If you can show special circumstances, they might be prepared to overrule their planning officers, as an exception to normal policies. Another possibility is simply to wait – there could be changes

in circumstances in the future that would make your proposal acceptable to the council, such as new buildings erected nearby, new planning policies or a change in policy boundaries. The other way to overcome a refusal on principle is to appeal (see Part Three). When planning permission is granted, but the conditions are unacceptable, you have three options: ignore them, appeal against them, or make a planning application to remove them. Ignoring conditions can have serious consequences (see Chapter 9). If the condition is fundamental to the permission, an appeal could result in you losing it altogether. The safest option is to apply to remove unacceptable conditions. Unless you can convince the council the condition is an unreasonable one, your application will be refused but you then have the option to appeal without the risk of losing the whole permission.

How best to deal with a refused planning permission or unacceptable conditions, and your chances of achieving a successful outcome, are difficult questions. Some finely balanced judgements might be needed and you can get into quite complex areas of law, policy and procedure. Getting advice from a planning consultant at this point

PLANNING APPLICATION ACTION CHECKLIST

1 decide what you want to do

2 decide what help you need, such as planning consultant and building designer

3 prepare or commission a sketch scheme

4 discuss your proposal with a planning officer

5 find out what application documents are required

6 review your proposal in light of the planning officer's comments

7 carry out any other pre-application consultations

8 commission application drawings and any statements/reports required

9 obtain and complete planning application forms

10 write or commission a supporting letter/planning statement

11 check the planning application fee

12 submit the application to the council

13 check the council's acknowledgement letter or contact the council if the letter doesn't arrive within a week

14 read letters and consultee responses

15 check progress of the application with the planning officer

16 submit further information and/or revise the application, if necessary

17 read the planning officer's report (committee decision)

18 contact councillor (committee decision)

19 attend committee meeting and speak, if appropriate

20 study decision notice

21 if approved, apply for approval of reserved matters or to discharge conditions

22 if refused, consider re-applying and/or appealing the decision

Figure 8.6

could save you time, trouble and money.

COMPLAINTS

Councils have complaints procedures and you can find out about these and how to make a complaint from the council's website or from their offices. You can also complain to the Ombudsman if you feel the council handled your planning application particularly badly, treated you unfairly or failed to follow procedure properly. Complaints are made to the Local Government Ombudsman (England), the Scottish Public Services Ombudsman, the Public Services Ombudsman for Wales or the Assembly Ombudsman for Northern Ireland. The Ombudsman can't change the decision and maladministration is found in only a small fraction of cases – very few are investigated beyond the preliminary stage. You can get information on making a complaint from the Local Government Ombudsman website or Citizens Advice Bureau.

CHAPTER 9

DEVELOPMENT WITHOUT PERMISSION

B uilding work and changes of use should have planning permission before they're carried out and authorised work should be carried out in line with the permission and its conditions. In this chapter we look at what can happen if work goes ahead without permission or not in accordance with permission. Councils have various ways of dealing with unauthorised development and these are collectively called 'enforcement'. Unauthorised development isn't a criminal offence but, where a council takes enforcement action which isn't complied with, the offender can be prosecuted and fined. Exceptions are work on Listed Buildings and Tree Preservation Order trees and demolition in a Conservation Area without the appropriate permission, which are automatically criminal offences.

NEED FOR PERMISSION

When you want to carry out work and aren't sure whether planning permission is needed, speak to a planning officer. He or she might ask for a sketch, or come to your property to have a look. Whether a planning application is required isn't always straightforward as some things, like minor works and repairs, don't need planning permission at all. Work could be covered by an existing permission and other items of work come within the 'permitted development' rules, which can be complex (see Chapter 2). If your project is large and you're told permission isn't needed, at least ask for written confirmation. You wouldn't be able to rely on what an officer allegedly said on the phone, if action was taken when the work had been done. Get professional advice if you're not satisfied with what the planning officer says. There's a formal way to establish whether work you intend to carry out, or have carried out, needs permission. This is done by making an application for a Lawful Development Certificate. The procedure is like a planning application but the main difference is that the council is supposed to decide the application only on the basis of the law – whether it likes the project shouldn't be considered

(although in practice it could influence the decision). Usually it's easier to make a planning application if the planning officer tells you one is needed. Make a Lawful Development Certificate application instead where you believe permission isn't required and where the council would: refuse a planning application; put unacceptable conditions on a planning permission; or take enforcement action if you just went ahead with the work. After certain time limits, the council can't take action against unauthorised development. In simple terms, these are: four years for building works and using a building to live in; and ten years for changes of use and breaking planning conditions.

ENFORCEMENT PROCEDURE

The council has a number of weapons to use against unauthorised development. In practice, you'd be contacted by a planning officer or the council's enforcement officer, often as a result of a complaint by a member of the public. The officer normally inspects the site and talks to you about what's been done. Co-operate with him as it's

LETTER FROM THE COUNCIL ABOUT
UNAUTHORISED DEVELOPMENT

RUSTON BOROUGH COUNCIL

Mr R Hapliss
171 Station Road
Redbrick
Bozeshire RE5 1SS
Date: 19th May 2009

Our ref: EN/09/023
Your ref:
Contact: Denzel Crush
Direct line: 01367 900762

Dear Mr Hapliss

TOWN & COUNTRY PLANNING ACT 1990
171 STATION ROAD, REDBRICK

I refer to the inspection of your property made by my Investigation Officer Denzel Crush on 8th May 2009.

It appears that a timber building has been erected at the side of your house and this building is being used, together with the garage and driveway of the property, for the storage of materials and the parking of vehicles in connection with the carrying on of a business, namely carpentry and/or decorating.

The council is of the opinion that the timber building requires planning permission and that, in respect of the part business use, a material change of use has taken place also requiring planning permission. I can find no record of any planning application or planning permission for either the building or change of use. I therefore suggest, if you wish the building to remain and the part business use to continue, that you make a planning application to this authority forthwith. I cannot, of course, pre-judge what decision the council would make on any such planning application you may submit.

Should the building remain and the use continue and no planning application is forthcoming, I will report the matter to the Director of Planning and Environment who may decide to authorise the taking of appropriate enforcement action.

Yours sincerely

C Spanner

Craig Spanner, Director of Planning and Environment

Figure 9.1

Where the council believes unauthorised development has taken place they usually write inviting you to make a planning application

the officers who largely decide whether to take further action and you won't be doing yourself any favours if you're hostile. In any event, the council can serve an official notice on you to get all the information it wants. Either at a meeting on site or in a letter sent afterwards (see Figure 9.1 opposite), the officers will tell you what you should do. This could be to take steps to remedy the unauthorised development or to make a planning application. They might at the same time say whether permission is likely to be granted. Councils aren't meant to ask for a planning application just because work should have had permission and there's supposed to be a good reason, such as that they believe conditions are necessary. Discuss the situation with the officer – you might be able to negotiate a solution – or try talking to councillors. If it looks like planning permission would be granted, make a planning application. Or, where there's a lot at stake, such as the possibility of taking down buildings, speak to a planning consultant. If you don't stop work, rectify what you've done or make a planning application, and the council doesn't

drop the matter, it might take enforcement action. In most cases, this involves the council serving an enforcement notice setting out what it says the unauthorised development is, what you must do about it and how long you have to do it.

Treat any notice you get very seriously – there are strict time limits for you to act and prosecution in the courts can follow, if you fail to comply. If you receive an enforcement notice and want to dispute it, get professional advice immediately. You can appeal against an enforcement notice and all the time an appeal is running the notice is suspended, which means even if you lose, you don't have to comply until after the appeal decision has been made.

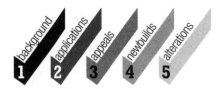

PART 3

MAKING A PLANNING APPEAL

A n appeal takes your planning application out of the hands of planning officers, councillors and local politics into the realms of more technical planning decisions. Here there's a timetable you must work to and ways of methodically proceeding, putting together a case and presenting information to give your appeal the very best chance of success. As a non-professional, in some less complicated cases, it can be possible to take on and win an appeal - if you understand the procedures, what sort of arguments will count and the right way to go about it. This section takes you through the process and shows you how to conduct your own appeal. Bear in mind there are minor differences in procedure between appeals in England, on which this Part is based, and those in Wales, Northern Ireland and, particularly, in Scotland.

appeals
3

CHAPTER 10

FIRST CONSIDERATIONS

You can appeal against a planning decision in the following circumstances:
■ refusal of planning permission or to approve reserved matters;
■ refusal of any other approvals required by a condition;
■ failure to decide your planning application within eight weeks of submission;
■ planning permission is granted but includes unacceptable conditions.

In England and Wales appeals are decided by inspectors from the Planning Inspectorate and, in Northern Ireland, by commissioners from the Planning Appeals Commission. In Scotland, appeals against planning committee decisions and Listed Building and Conservation Area consent decisions are decided by reporters from the Directorate for Planning and Environmental Appeals. Challenges to delegated decisions (decisions made by planning officers) go through a review process decided by a local review body made up of councillors (see below). Appeals are made by completing a form and sending it to the Planning Inspectorate or equivalent body in Northern Ireland and Scotland, within six months of the council's decision (three months in Scotland and 12 weeks in the case of householder appeals in England) but always double-check this deadline.

WHETHER TO APPEAL

First, think seriously about your chances of success: of all appeals made for all types of development, about a third are successful, the success rate for schemes of up to ten houses is about 30% and for other minor residential appeals the figure is under 40%. Appeals can be a lottery at the best of times and the odds, shown by the statistics, are against you from the outset, so take an objective look at your proposal. Appeals are supposed to be a last resort so weigh up carefully whether a revised application would be the better route. Read the decision notice and officer's report thoroughly, analysing each of the council's reasons for refusal or reasons for including a condition, because you need a convincing answer to each one. Reasons for refusal relate to detail, planning policies, technical standards and matters of opinion.

Points of detail, such as design and layout, can often be overcome by amending the application, so where you're prepared to make changes, a new application is probably better than appealing. If you want the proposal the way it is, think what points justify it, bearing in mind what the council said. The reasons will refer to planning policies so look up those policies to see whether there's a clear conflict with them or whether it's a matter of interpretation. If the reasons for refusal state that your application didn't comply with the council's technical standards, such as car parking spaces, distances between buildings or access arrangement, find out what the requirements are. If you can comply, make a new application. Where you can't, you need to show the standard is unreasonable, incorrectly applied or there are exceptional circumstances in your case that justify not complying. Matters of opinion are probably hardest to weigh up, especially when they relate to the appearance of buildings or the effect of a proposal on the character of an area. Planning officers make firm statements about such things, as if they were scientifically proven facts, but don't be put off – although experience comes into it, one person's opinion is as valid as another's. Planning is largely about matters of opinion and you can't predict the views of an appeal inspector.

Satisfy yourself on these points before going any further. Speak to the planning officer about an appeal; some will try to put you off but others will give you surprisingly candid advice. Ask whether similar proposals have been to appeal and get the addresses to look up at the planning department or search on the council's website. Study decisions to help you form a view on your application. Look particularly for points of principle and reasoning - the actual decision might be immaterial. Council's can refuse to consider similar applications in certain circumstances but this doesn't apply to genuine attempts to overcome objections to previous applications. Clarify this with a planning officer, if necessary.

In appeals, the appellant and the council are expected to pay their own costs and for you that would include any professional fees you incur. However, inspectors and reporters do have the power to award costs against either party in an appeal for what's called 'unreasonable behaviour' (but not in written appeals in Wales or any appeals in Northern Ireland). Examples of this could include putting forward a large amount of new material that should have been provided at the application stage, failing to turn up for a site inspection, withdrawing the appeal or making an appeal which had no chance of success. The latter might apply to cases where the proposal is clearly against planning policy, especially in the Green Belt, without justification, there's a recent dismissed appeal for a very similar scheme on the site or no legal agreement is provided where one is obviously needed. It's open to you to claim costs against the council if it doesn't back up its reasons for refusal or turns down an application which plainly should have been approved. Costs are awarded in less than one in ten appeals but it might be worth getting a professional opinion before embarking on an appeal (see below).

METHODS OF APPEAL

Appeals are dealt with in one of three ways - written, hearings and public inquiries/formal hearings. About 80% of appeals are decided by the written method, around 16% by hearings and about 4% by inquiries. Four parties get involved in appeals: you (the appellant); the council; the inspector; and members of the public. Appellants initially choose the method of appeal they would prefer but the Planning Inspectorate has the right to over rule that choice. The procedure for written appeals is shown in Figure 10.1 and involves you and the council drawing up statements which are exchanged and sent to the Planning Inspectorate. After this a site visit is made and the inspector writes a decision letter (see Figure 12.1). There is a slightly different procedure for householder appeals in England, which applies to extensions, alterations and outbuildings (see below).

Public inquiries take place where appeals are complex, issues need to be discussed, large numbers of people will take part or a lot of money is at stake. Inquiries aren't usually held for single houses or minor residential work but are not unknown. The appellant and council exchange statements and the inquiry itself is like an informal court hearing, with the inspector as the judge. The parties normally use barristers or solicitors and expert witnesses, such as planning consultants, engineers and landscape architects, and each presents its case and is questioned by the other side. A site inspection takes place and the inspector writes a decision letter. Inquiries can be daunting, as you have to contend with inquiry procedure and cross examination but, though professional representation can be expensive, inquiries do let you test the council's arguments thoroughly.

A hearing is a discussion between an inspector and the parties, of the contentious issues and is on a smaller scale than a public inquiry as neither party has the same sort of professional team. The appellant and council exchange statements beforehand and the hearing starts with the inspector summarising the cases and stating which issues he/she wants to discuss. Each side then has the opportunity to make its points and explain its views. Discussion about the appeal

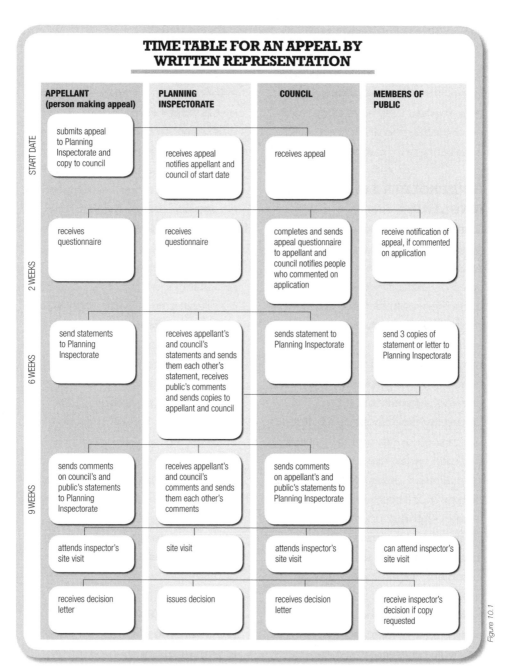

TIME TABLE FOR AN APPEAL BY WRITTEN REPRESENTATION

	APPELLANT (person making appeal)	PLANNING INSPECTORATE	COUNCIL	MEMBERS OF PUBLIC
START DATE	submits appeal to Planning Inspectorate and copy to council	receives appeal notifies appellant and council of start date	receives appeal	
2 WEEKS	receives questionnaire	receives questionnaire	completes and sends appeal questionnaire to appellant and council notifies people who commented on application	receive notification of appeal, if commented on application
6 WEEKS	send statements to Planning Inspectorate	receives appellant's and council's statements and sends them each other's statement, receives public's comments and sends copies to appellant and council	sends statement to Planning Inspectorate	send 3 copies of statement or letter to Planning Inspectorate
9 WEEKS	sends comments on council's and public's statements to Planning Inspectorate	receives appellant's and council's comments and sends them each other's comments	sends comments on appellant's and public's statements to Planning Inspectorate	
	attends inspector's site visit	site visit	attends inspector's site visit	can attend inspector's site visit
	receives decision letter	issues decision	receives decision letter	receive inspector's decision if copy requested

Figure 10.1

Written appeals are conducted according to a timetable with which you must comply

and this is the timetable for England and Wales

can continue at the hearing site visit, unlike the other methods where the site visit is purely an inspection. Hearings are a more user-friendly way of making your points in person and challenging the planning officer about his case.

HOUSEHOLDER APPEAL SERVICE (ENGLAND)

This is a streamlined appeal method for domestic planning application appeals in England, which is used for works such as extensions, alterations, garages, outbuildings, swimming pools, accesses, walls and fences. It's not used where new units would be created, for work on flats, for appeals against conditions, for Listed Building consent appeals, when the council hasn't made a decision within eight weeks or for complicated cases. A householder appeal must be made within 12 weeks of the council's decision so you need to act quickly. There's a specific appeal form to complete, which includes your grounds of appeal saying exactly why permission should be given, similar to a written appeal, and you only have to attach copies of the application form and the council's decision notice. The

council provides the remaining application documents and a completed questionnaire. The inspector makes a decision based just on the information the council had when it made its decision, the grounds of appeal and the council's questionnaire, which it submits within five working days. No other representations can be made, including by objectors or supporters. The inspector visits the site alone unless the appellant or neighbours have to be present to provide access to private land but no discussion of the case takes place. The decision is supposed to be sent out within eight weeks of the start of the appeal. If the appellant or the council doesn't think the case is suitable for this simplified process, they can say so when submitting the form or application information and questionnaire and the Planning Inspectorate decides the issue. There's nothing to stop you using a professional to make your householder appeal.

LOCAL REVIEW PROCESS (SCOTLAND)

In Scotland, like the rest of the UK, councils decide what types of planning application can be decided by planning officers and which must go to the planning committee for determination. Delegated decisions in Scotland can't be appealed to the Directorate for Planning and Environmental Appeals but can only be reviewed. The local review process is similar to an appeal but the decision is made by a committee of at least three councillors acting as the local review body. A notice of review has to be submitted to the council within three months of the delegated decision or failure of the officer to make a decision within two months of validation of the planning application. The notice must include the reasons for requesting the review, all documents the applicant wishes to put forward and what procedure the applicant wants. The precise arrangements for reviews are decided by each council and the local review body can dictate which procedure is appropriate. If the local review body believes it has sufficient information it can just make its decision but where it feels more detail is needed it can ask for written submissions, specifying a date by which this has to be provided, hold a hearing or carry out a site inspection, which can take place at any stage in the process. In more complicated cases, a pre-examination meeting can be held. New material can't be introduced in a review unless it wasn't available at the planning application stage or there are exceptional circumstances. If a hearing is held, the local review body specifies which issues it wishes to discuss and only those matters can then be raised at the hearing. The local review body issues a decision notice giving its determination and the reasons for making the decision.

GETTING PROFESSIONAL HELP

If you're thinking seriously about going to appeal (or local review, in Scotland) your project must be important to you. Whilst personal qualities can count at the planning application stage, appeals are more technical and decided on planning merits alone. If you make an appeal yourself, use the written procedure and don't attempt an inquiry without any advice. Most building surveyors, architects, and solicitors who make planning applications won't handle appeals but get in specialist planning consultants who are mainly chartered planning

Where a council refuses permission because of local objection an appeal is likely to be necessary, as happened in this case in which costs were awarded against the council for not producing sound evidence

and development surveyors or chartered town planners. Surveyor planning consultants have a wide understanding of property, including valuation, and usually a background in private practice, whereas town planners work mainly in local government although many leave to act as consultants. Ask other professional advisors to recommend a consultant or look in Yellow Pages under 'Planning Consultants'.

Cost is, of course, a consideration with professional help, so get a quotation, having satisfied yourself that the consultant has the right experience and knowledge for your case. Appeals are always a gamble but using a consultant increases your prospects of winning, so relate the cost of advice to the value and importance of your proposal when deciding whether to get professional help.

CHAPTER TEN ● FIRST CONSIDERATIONS

CHAPTER 11

PREPARING FOR AN APPEAL

Appeal forms are available from The Planning Inspectorate, Directorate for Planning and Environmental Appeals in Scotland or, for Northern Ireland, the Appeals Commission, either via the websites or by phone order. Appeals can be completed and lodged on line or using paper copies. The forms are slightly different for each country but the information required is similar. Appeal forms come with guidance notes and all the certificates and notices you might need. Make sure you have the planning application and council's decision notice to hand when you fill in the form.

COMPLETING THE APPEAL FORM

The name of appellant you give should be the same as shown on the application form, as only the person who made the application can appeal. If the application wasn't made in your name, get the written consent of the applicant to make the appeal. If you use consultants, they'll usually complete the form, entering their name here as your 'agent'. Correspondence then takes place with them. Information about the council and application can be taken from the planning application and decision notice. An Ordnance Survey grid reference of the site is asked for and the planning department should be able to help if you have trouble with this. If you're appealing on-line, the Planning Portal website has a facility to find the grid reference for you. You have to indicate what type of council decision your appeal is against. Again, where the answer isn't immediately clear, the planning officer can clarify the point.

The critical section is the grounds of appeal, about which you need to think most carefully - everything else on the form is simply factual. With written appeals you're supposed to submit your full case or statement along with the appeal form (see following section). You can add to this later but there are strictly enforced time limits for the submission of statements and other appeal documents (see Figure 10.1 on page 131). With hearings and inquiries you can

provide in the grounds of appeal section an outline of your main arguments, taking a paragraph for each. Look at the council's reasons for refusal (or reasons for imposing a condition) and deal with each of these stating why they're incorrect or why they don't justify the refusal of planning permission. Concentrate primarily on answering the council's objections but you can include other points in favour of your proposal, remembering that the inspector is only interested in proper planning points. Example grounds of appeal are given in Figure 11.2 on page 140. Make your grounds of appeal as comprehensive as possible as you're not supposed to bring up completely new arguments later on. Appeal forms in Northern Ireland don't ask for grounds of appeal.

You have to indicate which method of appeal you would prefer and are given a choice of the three: written, hearing or inquiry. Mostly you get your preferred option, although the Planning Inspectorate can dictate the method. There are ownership and agricultural certificates within the appeal form. Complete these just as you did for the planning application (see Chapter 7) so, if you're not the owner, you must serve a notice on owners and tenants telling them about the appeal. The certificates require a separate signature. There's a useful check list of the documents you'll need to enclose with the appeal form. You're asked for a plan showing the location of the site and you can use the relevant part of a 1:10,000 Ordnance Survey plan or street plan, marking the site in red. If you don't understand which documents are required, phone the Planning Inspectorate or ask a planning officer. Write out a full list of all the documents you're sending with the appeal and attach that list to the other papers. Finally, sign and date the form, and if you have to serve a notice on an owner or tenant, complete that as well. There's a fee to pay for making an appeal in Northern Ireland.

APPEAL STATEMENTS

The statement is your opportunity to influence the decision. There's no set form for these – the length, detail and content are entirely up to you – although the Planning Inspectorate does give guidance on presentation of documents.

When the issues are very straightforward you could just rely on relatively brief points which you would include in the grounds of appeal section of the appeal form. We set out a suggested structure for a comprehensive appeal statement here but not all the areas have to be covered - this will depend on the size and type of project. The general guidance for writing letters in support of your planning application (see Chapter 7) is relevant here and the two most important points to remember are that the information should be clear and relevant. Remember too to be careful to avoid putting in substantial new research or information which could have been included at the application stage. Apart from the application documents and council's questionnaire, the inspector only knows what he's told about the appeal in the statements and what he sees for himself at the site visit, so your objective is to supply all the facts that'll lead him to the conclusion that permission should be granted.

INTRODUCTION

Set out very briefly what the appeal is about: what the planning application was for, address of the site and council's decision. Describe your application: its date, what information, if any, accompanied it (illustrative drawings, covering letter or specialist's report) and amendments made. Then describe the council's decision on the planning application: planning officer's recommendation, date of committee meeting or decision and reasons given for refusal or for conditions. The inspector has all this information anyway but it helps to set the scene.

LOCATION AND DESCRIPTION

Inspectors have only a short time to see the appeal site and its surroundings when making site visits and the inspector who decides your appeal won't live or work in the area. In this section describe physical features of the area relevant to the appeal, particularly those which help your case. Start with a brief description of where the site is located in relation to main roads and facilities and the district, town or village. Go on to describe the appeal site itself: its area and dimensions, existing buildings and existing use, characteristics – slope,

APPEAL FORM HEADINGS

A Appellant details
B Agent details for the appeal (if any)
C Local Planning Authority (LPA) details
D Appeal site address
E Description of the development
F Reasons for the appeal
G Choice of procedure
      The written representations procedure
      The hearing procedure
      The inquiry procedure
H Grounds of appeal
I (part one) Appeal site ownership details
      (part two) Agricultural holdings certificate
J Essential supporting documents
K Other appeals
L Check sign and date
M Now send
N Appeal documents

Figure 11.1

Planning appeal forms require you to provide information under these main section headings; these are the headings from the on-line appeal form for England and Wales

trees, ground, site boundaries – and access arrangements. Then describe the surrounding properties: nature of uses, size, design, age and style of buildings, size and character of plots, windows facing appeal site, existing screening, public roads – type, level of use, pavements,

GROUNDS OF APPEAL

Provision can be made for access, visibility splays, turning and parking in line with the highway authority's Design Standards for New Accesses 2007. There is no objection from the highway authority.

The trees to be felled are not significant and remaining trees would be unaffected by the proposed building. New tree planting can be carried out and the character of the site will remain unchanged. There would be no conflict with policy LS9.

The proposal is consistent with Local Development Framework policy. The site is within the defined Development Boundary and complies with the council's policies for the design and siting of new houses H7, H18 and H19.

Planning permission has already been granted for a house and the appeal proposal would be a more appropriate scheme for the site as it would be less prominent.

The pattern of development locally includes a wide variety of house and plot sizes. The appeal site is larger than many other plots in the vicinity and the size of house proposed is not out of keeping with surrounding development. It would comply with saved Local Plan policy DES12.

The design of the proposed building is compatible with other near-by properties in terms of its height, bulk, proportions, fenestration and use of materials as set out in Supplementary Planning Document SPD3: Design and Layout.

The scheme would not result in neighbouring properties being overlooked and there will be no loss of privacy for their occupants. There are existing trees and hedges on the site boundaries and these can to be retained.

Adequate space exists on the appeal site for the house, garage, access drive, parking and turning spaces and for private garden areas. There is a suitable gap between the proposed house and flank boundaries. The site layout is in accordance with Development Control Policies DC7 and DC12, and the council's design guidelines.

Figure 11.2

Grounds of appeal set out why you think permission should be given like these examples

verges, and any nearby public footpaths. Consider including a set of photos to aid the inspector's memory and to help make your points.

PLANNING HISTORY

Previous decisions are sometimes mentioned in the planning officer's report on the application, but don't rely on this because the planning history might be quoted selectively. Look up the planning record at the council's offices and, if there are previous applications or appeals for similar schemes, ask for the files. Find the planning officer's report and the decision notice and note any useful points, including the date of decision and application reference number. If you come across a very helpful decision – such as an earlier permission for the same type of development – buy a photocopy to include in your statement. Carry out the same exercise for other sites; look around the area to see where new houses, extensions or conversions have been built recently and research these sites in the same way. In your statement, describe any other relevant planning applications, including the address, drawing

attention to positive points which apply in your case.

PLANNING POLICIES

There are several potential sources of relevant planning policy – government advice, district council documents and supplementary council guidance – and you can see all these on-line or at the planning department. The officer's report and decision notice might refer to planning policies and the planning officers should be able to tell you what guidance and policies apply to your proposal. After the appeal gets underway, the council will send you photocopies of the planning policies to which it will refer. You can deal with just these if you want to but there could be others which are more helpful. Study planning policies carefully and read the text which explains them. In this section of your statement you should mention the policies you think should be taken into account in the decision. A list can be sufficient. Give the name of the plan or document and policy reference numbers, and quote important parts of the policies, print off or photocopy pages from a plan to attach to your statement – apart from government advice,

STREET SCENE DRAWING

No 21 | Existing No 23 | Appeal site with proposed house | No 25

Figure 11.3

A street-scene drawing shows how well a new building will fit in with its neighbours

the inspector won't have copies of the documents.

PLANNING ISSUES

In previous sections you'll have presented the facts – this is the part of your statement where you can bring everything together and put forward your arguments in support of the appeal. The issues to concentrate on are usually the ones raised in the decision notice. Councils' statements often mix facts, policy and opinion all together, so it can be difficult to identify separate specific issues in their cases. It's good discipline to start this section with a short list of what you think are the main issues, then go on to deal with each in turn. In your statement, try to show how your application is consistent with planning policies. Think too about the purpose of the policy, not about interpretations of the words which are too strict or literal. If your application conflicts with some aspect of a policy, give reasons why it shouldn't apply or state what's exceptional in your case, and counter this with policies which support your proposed development. Draw on the facts you've set out to reach conclusions supporting your proposal. Compare your site or property with others to demonstrate how your scheme is consistent and compatible and describe how the proposal would fit acceptably into the setting. Assess how much of the scheme could be seen from where and explain how insignificant that would be. Consider also what else is visible within the same aspect – next to, in front of and behind the property – and how that limits the impact of your scheme. Describe how the proposal blends with, or doesn't harm, the character of the existing building or of the area. All of this can be backed up effectively with the inclusion of photographs, plans and drawings (see Figure 11.3 on the facing page). For example:

■ plan showing all sites where similar applications have been permitted;

■ plan marking houses that have similar size plots;

■ plan indicating the only public places from which the building could be seen;

■ drawing showing the proposed building in relation to adjoining houses;

■ drawings illustrating how a building could fit on the site (outline applications).

appeals
3

CHAPTER 12
CONDUCTING THE APPEAL

Having completed the appeal form and your full statement, if you decide to prepare a separate one, you're ready to lodge the appeal. If you lodge the appeal on-line, you can send the accompanying documents electronically or post paper copies. You also need to print off the appeal form to send to the council. If you complete a paper form, take at least two copies of that and the statement and list of documents you're sending with it. Keep one full copy for yourself and send a copy of the form to the council (the council doesn't need copies of the application documents; the list is sufficient). Send to the Planning Inspectorate, Directorate for Planning and Environmental Appeals or Planning Appeals Commission: the appeal form, your statement, the list of documents enclosed and copies of the documents themselves. If you do have to give notice of the appeal to owners or tenants, do this at the same time as you send in the forms and include a letter inviting them to contact you if they want more information or have questions. The Planning Inspectorate writes acknowledging the appeal, confirming the method to be used and giving the official starting date for the appeal timetable, which is the date of its letter. The procedure and timetable is summarised in the letter and you must comply with it – failure to comply results in documents being returned unseen by the inspector. If you can get support for your appeal from people who live close by, urge them to write to the Planning Inspectorate in favour of your proposal, giving them the address to write to, the appeal reference number and the deadline (six weeks). It's essential that such letters, in order to be effective, concentrate on planning issues, so make sure your supporters are quite clear on what the issues are in the case and which points aren't relevant. For example, if one of the reasons for refusal was the anticipated effect on occupiers of adjoining houses, try to get the neighbours to write stating why they feel your proposal wouldn't cause them any harm.

RE-APPLYING TO THE COUNCIL

When your appeal is underway, you could consider making a revised planning application. Remember that councils can sometimes refuse to consider follow up applications so discuss this with a planning officer to avoid wasting time. You can appeal if the council doesn't decide your application within eight weeks so, if the council drags its feet, you could think about making a planning application for an alternative scheme and get an appeal going to help focus the council's attention. Do though check with the planning officer that the council considers the revised application is sufficiently different to avoid it using its power not to consider similar applications. Never withdraw an appeal unless your second planning application is actually permitted and get the council's agreement to withdrawal to avoid a cost claim. Even when permission is granted, you can let the appeal run and, if successful, you have the choice of which permission to carry out.

APPEAL QUESTIONNAIRE

The council sends you and the Planning Inspectorate a

completed appeal questionnaire, setting out information about the application and site. Check whether the council agrees to the written procedure; if it doesn't, this means an inquiry or hearing might be held and you should get professional advice. Councils are usually happy to go along with a written appeal – it involves less work and avoids the rigours of a hearing and public inquiry. The questionnaire says how many responses to consultation the council received at the application stage – parish council's views, highway authority comments and letters from local residents. Copies of these responses, together with relevant extracts from planning documents should be attached to the questionnaire. Check the information given in the questionnaire and read all the attached papers. If they contain points you haven't covered or new information helpful to your case, you can write again, within the six week deadline, adding to your grounds of appeal or statement.

COUNCIL'S STATEMENT AND LETTERS

The council has to send two copies

of its statement to the Planning Inspectorate within six weeks and one copy is forwarded on to you. Occasionally, councils elect not to submit a statement but rely on the planning officer's report on the planning application and on the policy documents. You have to submit any comments you want to make on the council's statement within nine weeks of the appeal start date which, in theory, should give you three weeks to respond. However, because the Planning Inspectorate is sometimes slow in sending on statements, in practice, you might well not have a full three weeks. You must still meet the nine-week deadline unless the Planning Inspectorate extends the period in its covering letter. Read a statement very carefully – check the facts are accurate, note the issues raised and how they're dealt with, see how each reason for refusal is backed up, and study the interpretation of planning policies. This can help refine your views and highlight what you must deal with in your response. Don't feel you must answer and reject every single point – merely saying you disagree will carry no weight at all. The council's statement might contain points that hadn't previously occurred to you, so there could be additional research to do. For example, the planning officer might refer to other planning decisions, particular view points or the level of traffic on the road. Your response could be to look at the other sites and distinguish them from yours, to visit the view points and make your own assessment or to assess whether the amount of traffic causes any problems.

In its statement, the council suggests conditions that it believes should be attached to planning permission, if it's granted. This is standard practice and doesn't imply the council thinks it's going to lose the appeal. Read the conditions and, if you don't understand them, speak to a planning officer. Where you feel the suggested conditions would be too restrictive or unjustified, say so in your comments on the council's case, and give your reasons. You can put forward your own suggestions for conditions that are acceptable to you and which might help limit the effects of your proposal, such as a condition requiring the planting of trees. Comments can be submitted via

the Planning Inspectorate website or by post, making sure you send two copies to arrive within nine weeks of the start date.

The people who wrote to the council about the original application are told of the appeal, but anyone else is also entitled to write at the appeal stage. These letters must be sent to the Planning Inspectorate within six weeks. Any letters about the appeal sent to the council are forwarded to the Planning Inspectorate. You're sent copies of all letters the inspector will see from whatever source along with the council's case and you have the right to respond to them within nine weeks of the appeal start date. Most letters are written by local objectors and are rarely effective but you might be surprised, and possibly offended, by the tone of the letters. Unless they raise sound planning issues which the council hasn't mentioned, don't respond to them – it might take enormous self control but it's in the best interests of your appeal. The inspector won't be swayed by the number of objections nor by non-planning factors, such as neighbour disputes (see Chapter 4), and by

EXAMPLE APPEAL DECISION LETTER

Site visit made on 20 January 2009
by Clarence Sparkey
an inspector appointed by the Secretary of
State for Communities and Local Government

Decision date:
26 January 2009

Appeal ref: APP/J7593/A/08/3478610
Land adjoining Petunia View, London Road, Bricklestick SD7 2NJ
• The appeal is made under Section 78 of the Town and Country Planning
  Act 1990 against a refusal to grant outline planning permission.
• The appeal is made by Mr & Mrs H Grant against Blocking District Council
• The application (Ref BC/08/2756), dated 4 July 2008 was refused by
  notice dated 5 September 2008.
• The development proposed is described as outline erection of a
  detached house.

Decision
1 I allow the appeal and grant outline planning permission for erection
of a detached dwelling at Land adjoining Petunia View, London Road,
Bricklestick SD7 2NJ, in accordance with the terms of the application
[Ref BC/08/2756] dated 4 July 2008 and the plans submitted therewith,
subject to the following conditions:

1) Details of the access, appearance, landscaping, layout and scale
(hereinafter called the 'reserved matters') shall be submitted to
and approved in writing by the local planning authority before any
development begins and the development shall be carried out as approved.

2) Application for approval of the reserved matters shall be made to the
local planning authority before the expiration of three years from the
date of this permission.

3) The development hereby permitted shall begin before the expiration of
two years from the date of approval of the last of the reserved matters
to be approved.

4) The development hereby permitted shall not begin until details of
the junction between the access to the site and London Road have been
approved in writing by the local planning authority and that junction
has been constructed in accordance with the approved details.

5) The dwelling hereby permitted shall not be occupied until works for
the drainage and disposal of surface water and sewage have been provided
on the site in accordance with details to be submitted to and approved
in writing by the local planning authority.

An appeal decision letter gives the inspector's reasons for the decision

Main Issues

2 I consider the main issues are a) the effect upon the character and appearance of this part of Bricklestick, b) the effect on the residential amenity of neighbours and c) whether a suitable access can be provided.

Reasons

3 The site forms part of the side garden of Petunia View and, being in a residential area, the principle of residential development is consistent with Local Plan policy H6. I saw during my visit that plot sizes in the vicinity are varied and, bearing in mind advice in PPS3 concerning efficient use of land, I do not consider that one dwelling on this site would be over-development. The formation of the new access will necessitate the removal of some hedging but I do not consider that this will cause unacceptable harm to the character or appearance of the area.

4 The appeal site has a common boundary with Homeleak, which is itself situated close to the boundary. There would be some effect on its residential amenities due to the normal noise and activity of domestic occupation. However, I am not convinced that this would be of such magnitude as to justify refusal and would accord with the criteria in Local Plan policy H6.

5 London Road has a speed limit of 30 mph and is a well used route between Brickstick and Trosset. In accordance with Manual for Streets visibility splays of 2.4 x 43 metres should be provided. This can be achieved to the east but only 39 metres is available to the west owing to the curve in the road. You point out that, as the appeal site is situated on the south side of London Road, traffic approaching from the west comes into view at a point 50 metres from the proposed access point. In view of this and the generally slow moving nature of the traffic on this stretch of road, 1 am satisfied that the access as proposed would not create an undue traffic hazard. In this regard, I conclude the proposal would not be harmful to highway safety and would not conflict with the aims and objectives of Structure Plan policy M3 and Local Plan policy TR8.

6 For the reasons given above and having regard to all other matters raised, I conclude that the appeal should be allowed. The council has suggested a number of conditions that should be attached to the permission if the appeal were allowed and I have adapted these using the model conditions suggested in circular 11/95.

Clarence Sparkey

INSPECTOR

Figure 12.1

149

responding to objection letters you can attach importance to them which is possibly more than they deserve.

SITE INSPECTION

Some time after the statements and comments on cases and letters have been exchanged, the Planning Inspectorate writes to you about the inspector's visit giving the time and date for the inspection and name and qualifications of the inspector. If you can't attend on the date given or find someone to go along for you, email or write back immediately saying so (but don't do this merely because the date isn't the most convenient for you). The inspector's qualifications give you an insight into his or her background but rarely provide clues to how he or she will view your proposal. Many inspectors are Members of the Royal Town Planning Institute (MRTPI), which usually means they've been planning officers for some or all of their careers before joining the Planning Inspectorate. Some inspectors are members of the Royal Institute of British Architects (ARIBA), trained in building design and might have definite ideas

about this. Other inspectors are Chartered Surveyors (MRICS) and civil engineers (MICE) which are practical professions.

On the day of the site visit, make sure you arrive early and have your papers with you in case the inspector has any questions. The inspector and planning officer arrive separately, as there's no contact between the inspector and the parties in an appeal (apart from during the inspection itself). Don't be surprised, therefore, if the inspector doesn't talk to you until the planning officer arrives. The inspector introduces him/ herself and makes a note of the name of everyone present, which can include any objectors who turn up but this isn't common. The inspector confirms he's got the correct drawings and then walks around the site and area observing and taking notes. You shouldn't try to discuss the merits of the proposal or put forward your arguments. You're only allowed to point out physical factors – where buildings would go, the position of boundaries, viewpoints, nearby buildings and other similar features. Work out in advance if there are particular physical features you want to point out

– otherwise, let the inspector walk around taking notes and be ready to answer his questions. Site inspections are invariably an anticlimax and most are over in 15 to 20 minutes, with scarcely a word spoken. Where possible inspectors make unaccompanied site visits when neither the appellant nor the council attend. This happens where the site can be seen clearly from public roads and the letter from the Planning Inspectorate would advise you if the inspection is to be unaccompanied.

THE DECISION

Once the inspector's site visit has taken place, there's nothing to do but wait for the decision letter which arrives anything between two and eight weeks afterwards. There's nothing to be gained by telephoning the Planning Inspectorate to find out where the decision has got to. Decision letters follow a common pattern, setting out the date when the inspector visited the site, the address of the site, the name of the council, the type of proposal and the decision. The inspector then says what he believes are the main issues, outlines the relevant planning policies, describes the site and surroundings and gives his views on the main issues. The inspector won't necessarily deal with every point you made and arguments you felt were convincing – the existence of a previous planning permission or the apparent lack of harm that would be caused – might not even be mentioned. The decision letter could leave you wondering exactly why your proposal was turned down, especially where the inspector lapses into planning jargon. An example of a decision letter is given in Figure 12.1 on pages 148–149. Appeals are either allowed or dismissed, which amounts to granting or refusing permission in the same way that councils decide planning applications. The appeal decision letter is equivalent to a council's decision notice and an allowed appeal will include conditions.

CHALLENGES AND COMPLAINTS

Appeal decisions can be challenged in the courts within six weeks of the decision but only on legal grounds – that the inspector acted outside his or her authority or you were prejudiced by the failure to follow correct procedure. You can't challenge a decision on the planning merits of the case or because you disagree with the inspector's opinion. Only a small fraction of all appeal decisions are challenged and, even when successful, the appeal has to be decided afresh and the original decision can be confirmed. The cost of taking such a step can run to tens of thousands of pounds, so consult a solicitor experienced in planning work before considering a legal challenge. If you believe the inspector didn't treat you fairly, you can contact the Quality Assurance Unit at the Planning Inspectorate; in Scotland, the Directorate Manager at the Directorate for Planning and Environmental Appeals; or in Northern Ireland, the Chief Administrative Officer at the Planning Appeals Commission. If you were unfairly treated through maladministration, including failure to follow proper procedures, you can complain to the Ombudsman. Complaints about national government, including agencies responsible for appeals, are made to the Parliamentary Ombudsman (only at the request of an MP), the Scottish Public Services Ombudsman, the Public Services Ombudsman for Wales

or the Assembly Ombudsman for Northern Ireland. None of these can question the merits of an appeal decision or change the result.

RE-SUBMISSION

A favourable appeal decision isn't necessarily the end of the line; where the original application was in outline you need to get the reserved matters approved (see Chapter 7), or you might decide to revise the scheme because, having established the right to carry out your project, you're in a stronger bargaining position with the council. Similarly, a dismissed appeal isn't always the end of your proposal, depending on whether the decision was made on points of principle, or detail, or technicalities. Occasionally, an inspector sets out his or her objections quite specifically and it's clear what amendments could make the scheme more acceptable. Try to overcome the inspector's objections by changing the design or layout, such as reducing the scale, making different access arrangements or other amendments. Appeal decisions aren't always clear and the planning officer might put a more restrictive interpretation on it than you. Where there's scope to revise a proposal, go back through the planning process again, with the pointers from the appeal decision firmly in mind. If a planning application is made for the same, or very similar scheme within two years of a dismissed appeal, the council can refuse to decide it. This isn't, however, supposed to prevent genuine attempts to get permission for a revised application.

HEARINGS

You or the council can ask for a hearing, and in exceptional cases the Planning Inspectorate might insist on one being held. Hearings in Scotland are rare. In any event the Planning Inspectorate tells you if an informal hearing is to take place and sends you a set of guidance notes. This method of appeal is similar to a written representations appeal. You aren't obliged to send your full case with the notice of appeal but you and the council still have to submit statements within six weeks of the start date and comment on each other's cases after nine weeks. The hearing will be held at the council's offices or

at a public building near the site. You should take along all your papers on the application and the appeal. In preparation for the hearing, look through the council's statement and make a note of counter arguments to the planning officer's points. The inspector explains the format, introduces the appeal, summarises the two sides' cases and outline the areas he or she wishes to discuss. You and the planning officer have the opportunity to deal with the points the inspector identifies and you'll both probably be asked questions by the inspector. Any members of the public who are present are also given an opportunity to say their piece. When the discussion at the hearing ends everyone attends the site inspection and, unlike a written representations site visit, discussion is sometimes allowed to continue and the inspector will take the lead in this.

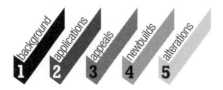

PART 4:

PLANNING PERMISSION FOR NEW HOMES

Getting planning permission is a fundamental part of building a new home. A refusal can cause months of delay, jeopardise the purchase of a building plot, or stop the whole project. Planning isn't an exact science. Local planning policies for house building vary and, ultimately, each application should be judged on its merits. Local politics has its role to play and consequently not all decisions are consistent. To ensure something as important as your future home gets fair consideration, you need to be aware of how the planning system works in relation to applications for new houses. This section, therefore, explains the factors the council will look at in an application and shows you what you can do to maximise your chances of success.

CHAPTER 13

SITE CONSIDERATIONS

Every potential site for a new home is different – each has its own constraints and opportunities which influence how, whether and where a house can be built. In this chapter we look at how these physical and legal factors affect the development of a building plot, and consequently, the prospects for getting planning permission on it. These factors, also known as 'site specific' considerations, are:

■ size and shape;
■ topography, or lie of the land;
■ flood risk;
■ ground conditions;
■ orientation;
■ trees and vegetation;
■ wildlife;
■ services;
■ access;
■ existing use;
■ legal constraints.

SIZE AND SHAPE

The size and shape of a plot is fundamental, because you must be able to fit the house, garage, parking and turning areas and

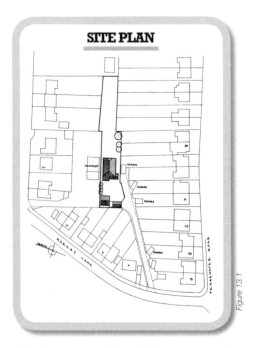

SITE PLAN

Figure 13.1

New house screened by workshop, garages and new tree planting; windows face front and rear gardens to avoid overlooking back gardens; shape of house designed to fit shape of plot

private garden space into it. Think carefully about designing a layout where all these elements fit together, especially where the plot is small or an awkward shape. Before you work up a plot layout, it's essential to get an accurate plan of the site. Even if you have a scale plan, it's worth taking check measurements yourself of crucial dimensions, such as the plot frontage. On a particularly awkward site you might need to employ a land surveyor to draw up an accurate plan with ground levels marked. Once you have an accurate scale plan, you can experiment with different site layouts by cutting out scale 'footprints' of your house and garage and moving them around on the plan. Try different shapes of house – an 'L' shape sometimes fits in where a rectangle wouldn't – and remember that garages can be detached, attached or integral (built into the house).

Councils look closely at site layouts when considering planning applications and tend to object if they're cramped. Some councils have their own design standards against which your scheme will be judged, covering factors such as distances between houses and minimum areas of private garden space. Your personal preferences, such as a tiny garden because you hate gardening or no garage because you don't drive, are given little credence by planning officers. On the whole, the smaller the plot, the smaller the house that will be permitted on it. An exception to this is urban infill plots, where a mews or terraced house sometimes occupies most, if not all, of the site. See Figures

Urban infill plot where the design will have to respect the size, style and privacy of adjoining houses

13.1 (opposite) and 13.2 (right) for examples of site layouts for plots with constraints. Figure 13.3 (above) illustrates a typical urban infill plot. If you try to get planning permission in your own garden, you'll have more control over the size and shape of the plot but you can't leave your existing home with inadequate garden or parking and turning space in order to maximise the size of the plot. Where a plot is sub-divided, the council will look closely at the layout of the existing house as well as at the new house and plot and permission can be refused if

New house positioned to avoid overlooking adjoining houses; staggered design to avoid losing trees; garage sited to screen house; new fence for privacy of existing house

the original would be left with an unsatisfactory layout.

TOPOGRAPHY

Not every house is built on level ground and sloping sites can often dictate the design and layout. Split-level designs and the use of retaining walls provide practical solutions but they might have visual implications unacceptable to the council, especially in sensitive areas such as Conservation Areas. In particular, you need to consider access arrangements carefully on sloping sites, as too steep a drive might result in vehicles grounding or can mean that cars are parked at a high level in relation to the road, so wouldn't be acceptable to the council. If you make a planning application on a sloping plot, include details of levels, ideally on cross-section drawings to show how level changes will be accommodated and how much cutting or filling is required.

Where a scheme has significant or complex level changes, a sketch or perspective drawing showing exactly how the finished scheme will look can be a worthwhile addition to your application plans. Reduce the impact of obtrusive retaining walls by specifying local materials and/or by landscaping and make sure you show such features in your drawings.

FLOOD RISK

Low-lying land and sites close to a watercourse or the sea can be liable to flooding. You can find out about this from the Environment Agency in England and Wales, the Rivers Purification Boards in Scotland or the Rivers Agency of the Department of Agriculture and Rural Development in Northern Ireland. Being in a flood zone can prevent you getting any kind of planning permission and you might be required by the council to commission an engineer to carry out a flood risk assessment to accompany your application. Where the risk is not overriding, setting ground floors above flood levels is obviously a practical necessity but can lead to objections from the council if the resulting design is unsatisfactory. Consult a building designer or engineer, or talk to a planning officer to get useful ideas for acceptable solutions to this problem.

GROUND CONDITIONS

Ground conditions could influence where you build on a plot and the

Figure 13.4

Building plot constrained by TPO tree, telegraph pole, change in levels and adjoining conservatory

type of foundations you need. In deciding planning applications, however, councils are interested in the design constraints on the house caused by poor ground conditions rather than the conditions themselves. One exception is contaminated land, as there might be a health risk – the council's environmental health department can advise you on this. Planning application forms don't ask questions about ground conditions but getting planning permission doesn't necessarily mean you'll get building regulations approval. If part of a plot is made-up, filled or unstable land, which is unsuitable for building, you should include a copy of a soil engineer's report with your planning application to support your case for building elsewhere on the plot. If the council wants the new house sited in an area that's unstable, they might be persuaded to accept an alternative siting, if you can prove this is impractical. Modern building techniques, however, now provide affordable solutions to nearly all ground condition problems.

BOUNDARIES

Application plans must show the

position of boundaries, so you need to identify these on site. Planning permission applies only to the site area defined on the application plans – where actual boundaries differ from those shown in an application, you might need to amend the permission or make a new application to regularise the position, before building can take place. If the exact position of a boundary is disputed with a neighbour, don't go into the details of this in your application – simply include all the land you believe you own within the red edging on your location plan. If the neighbour complains about this to the council, the worst that's likely to happen is that the planning officer will ask you to serve a formal notice of the application on your neighbour.

ORIENTATION

The orientation of a plot and a new house on it, is another factor which indirectly affects planning permission. Maximising natural light and thermal efficiency in a new home are often important design criteria and these factors influence the position of a house on a plot, the layout of rooms and the position of windows – all factors relevant to planning. However, in the face of other objections, the wider environmental benefits of an 'eco-friendly' home aren't likely to be given much weight by the council, unless it has a particularly 'green' bias.

TREES

Most councils are anxious to preserve trees and vegetation, and the position of these on a site often has a bearing on the planning permission you can get. Councils are concerned not just with the trees that are to be felled but also with likely demands to remove trees in future. For example, you might have every intention of keeping trees growing close to the back of your proposed home, as they provide shade and a woodland outlook, but the council will look at what typical occupiers would do and could conclude they would want to fell the trees to provide more light. Councils sometimes refuse planning permission because of the possibility of trees being cut down in future and the effect this would have on the landscape. If trees would be affected by your proposed building plans, taking a positive approach can overcome possible objections.

Where trees you would need to fell are over-mature, diseased or storm-damaged, make it clear in your letter accompanying the application. If possible, point out where replacement trees could be planted and include these on your site plan. Back up what you say with a report from a tree consultant (arboriculturist) or tree surgeon, ideally one who is experienced in dealing with your particular council.

Trees protected by Tree Preservation Orders (TPOs) or in a Conservation Area can be felled to make way for a house that has planning permission, as this overrides the protection but the trees to be cut down should be identified in the application drawings. Don't fell or damage other protected trees, as this is an offence for which you can be fined. Where TPO trees or trees in a Conservation Area have to be removed, take particular care to minimise the losses and show replacement planting wherever possible.

Sometimes trees create a problem where they block a view but also provide screening for an adjoining garden. Here, the council isn't interested in the view but in the potential loss of privacy. In such situations, and whenever trees affect how you build on a plot, there are three approaches to the problem. The first is the pre-emptive strike – decide where you want to site your house and simply cut down all the trees in the way (assuming they're not protected) before you make a planning application. This solves one problem, but can create others if the council's planning and landscape officers take a dim view or you incur the wrath of neighbours, stirring them to oppose your application. The second alternative is to negotiate with the council before you make a planning application. Invite the council's landscape officer (or planning officer, if they don't have one) to visit the site, talk enthusiastically about your desire to preserve the best trees and point out where replacements could be planted and ask for his or her advice, which, if possible, you then incorporate in your planning application. The third possibility is to just go ahead and make your planning application and let the loss of trees be one of the factors the council weighs up in assessing your proposal. Many councils routinely put TPOs on every tree on site as soon as they receive a planning application. This strengthens their position in negotiations over the site layout or the numbers of trees to be lost.

WILDLIFE

The council takes into account the effect on wildlife, particularly protected species, when assessing your application. If there's some indication that the site might be a habitat for wildlife, the council might ask for an ecological survey to establish exactly what's there. Some councils are quite zealous about this and insist you fill in a checklist to establish the likelihood of protected creatures living on your plot. The presence of badgers, for example, might be very obvious, but other species, such as reptiles or even rare beetles would be less so. The presence of protected species could hold up your project while measures are agreed either to accommodate them on site, or to relocate them during the appropriate season.

SERVICES

When you plan a new house, the position of services – electricity cables, gas mains, water pipes and sewers – can affect the layout, as the new building must connect to the services whilst avoiding the pipes and cables themselves. A main sewer usually has a 6 metre (19 feet) 'exclusion zone' and no building can take place in the strip 3 metres (10 feet) wide on either side of the sewer (see Figure 13.5 opposite). If the sewer is small, the council might allow building up to 2 metres (6 feet 8 inches) from the sewer, provided there's a 4 metre (13 feet) clear space on the other side. Where the position of services results in a poor site layout for your house, this can be a reason for refusing planning permission. Speak to the service provider and get confirmation in writing about what you can do over, under or near their apparatus. Show this to the planning officers to support your proposed layout.

Planning application forms also ask about foul and surface water drainage, although the council is only concerned that adequate drainage can be provided, not about how much it costs or whether it involves somebody else's land. Foul sewage is normally disposed of by a public foul sewer, private treatment system, septic tank or cesspit. The public sewer is generally the simplest and cheapest option but must be accessible and have adequate capacity. Where an alternative method is used, the council looks carefully at its implications.

A septic tank or a private disposal system must be located at least 5 metres (16 feet 6 inches) from the house and needs an area of land to drain into. The council consults the Environment Agency in England and Wales, the Rivers Purification Board in Scotland or the Water Management Unit in Northern Ireland about discharges into or near waterways, and these might not be permitted, or only from approved types of apparatus. Cesspits must be emptied, involving access for a heavy vehicle which can cause disturbance for neighbours or have access and highway safety implications. Find out which drainage method you'll use before

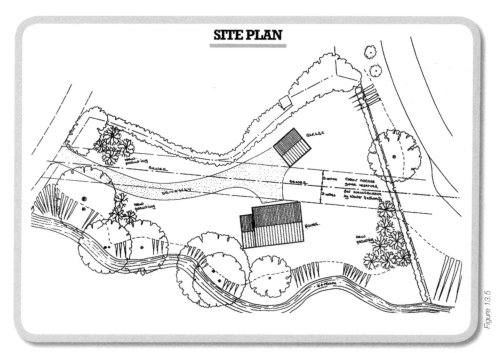

SITE PLAN

Figure 13.5

New house and garage positioned to avoid building over sewer and tree felling; new planting screens views into and out of site; wide footprint of house used to fit available building area and allow views into garden

making a planning application and whether it has any implications you need to take into account in working out a site layout.

Surface water is generally drained to soakaways, public surface water drains or to existing watercourses. The council might want proof, in the form of percolation tests, that soakaways would work on your site. Where they wouldn't, a lack of alternative means could lead to refusal of planning permission. Queries over foul and surface water disposal can cause delays with applications for new houses, so if you suspect difficulties, get advice from a building designer or drainage engineer before making your planning application.

ACCESS

Most new houses must have an access to a public highway and councils set standards covering access, parking and turning arrangements for new houses (see Chapter 7). District councils consult highway authorities about planning applications and, where highway standards aren't met, they can recommend that the council refuses the application. It's, therefore, important to know what

the standards are and to comply with them as far as possible. Standards vary depending on the type of road, and volume and speed of traffic, so you should ask the council what the requirements are in your particular circumstances. Where you can't meet the standards but there would be no significant threat to highway safety, the highway authority might not object to the application. Even where it does, the planning officer can ignore the recommendation, if he or she feels that the application is acceptable.

Visibility splays at access points (see Figure 7.3 on page 69) often cause difficulties where they would have to extend over someone else's land and you might have to get the agreement of a neighbour to cut back a hedge, move a fence or remove a tree. Bus shelters, telegraph poles, street trees and post boxes can all obstruct visibility and can be expensive or impossible to move, although telegraph poles, street lights and small trees are often tolerated within a visibility splay. Don't incur expense unless you're certain this is necessary. Planning permission is usually granted subject to a condition that the visibility splay is provided, so get permission first, then get the obstacle removed or negotiate the necessary agreement. If you can't meet highway standards, look for mitigating factors such as generally slow-moving or a very light flow of traffic in the road and point these out when you make your application. Where an existing access is being closed up or altered, check whether this would improve highway safety, as this might justify granting planning permission even though the new access is still below standard. Where you suspect there could be access issues, consider getting a highway consultant's advice or report to submit with your application.

Some house plots have an access to a private road, drive or track, the design of which often falls well below modern standards. The council might be reluctant to allow new building that increases the use of such a sub-standard road. Counter this, if you can, by showing that the road has an excellent safety record and to back up your claims obtain road traffic accidents reports from the local police. Consider also whether the road can be improved, as

other residents might be prepared to contribute to the cost. This demands a very careful public relations exercise, however, and a knowledge of who actually owns the road.

Houses to be built on 'backland' plots, where one house is built behind another, can create particular access problems – in most cases, the new drive will have to pass close to an existing house, so look for ways to minimise noise or disturbance, since this could be used as a reason for refusing your application. A 2 metre (6 feet 8 inches) close-board fence, between the existing house and the new drive, will help and, if there's space, a hedge planted on the house side of the fence will soften its appearance. If there's any choice in where the drive is positioned, keep it as far away from the house as possible but, if it must pass close to the house, try to choose a blank wall or a wall without windows to habitable rooms.

EXISTING USES

We've looked at the significance of the existing use of a site in getting planning permission (see Chapter 4).

165

Two level, clear plots with good road access in residential area

Where building a new house would improve a site, make sure you know precisely the nature and implications of the existing use so that this information can be used in support of the application. For example, if a use generates noise, identify who this affects and at what times of day. If the problem is smell, find out if the prevailing wind carries this towards or away from any adjoining houses. Where traffic is generated, record movements and check the accident records. Using such specific information on an existing use, you can show how the use of the site for a house will improve the situation. Such detailed information isn't appropriate in every case and sometimes the effects are best left to the planning officer's imagination, especially if you detect that his impression of the use is worse than the reality.

LEGAL MATTERS

Legal constraints to development, such as covenants and rights of way, aren't usually planning matters, although can affect planning permission in a variety of ways. If a covenant specifies that only a bungalow can be built on a plot, this doesn't stop the council granting planning permission for a two-storey house. A covenant

Figure 13.7

Spacious garden plot free from obstacles and not overlooked by neighbours

might have an indirect effect on planning permission, for example, because it influences the site layout. If a covenant prevents building on the part of the plot where the council would want the house, and alternative positions are unacceptable, the covenant could in effect bar development of the site. Councils are usually keen to protect the convenience and safety of public footpaths and bridleways and are likely to refuse permission if a new house would affect their use. If building your house involves diverting a public right of way, the grant of planning permission doesn't in itself mean the house can be built as a formal footpath diversion order is also required. Planning obligations/agreements (see Chapter 1) affecting single plots are uncommon, except those relating to the payment of financial contributions, but might have been drawn up by a previous owner in the process of getting an earlier permission. If this is the case, you'll have to comply with the terms as they're binding on all owners of a site. The existence of a planning obligation shows up on your property title deeds and the planning officer should draw your attention to it, if it affects your proposal.

newbuilds

4

CHAPTER 14

GENERAL CONSIDERATIONS

Planning permission for a new house is influenced by factors beyond the site considerations, which concern the practicalities of whether a house can be built and where. The general considerations we now look at determine how a new house will fit in, both with its surroundings and with the council's plans for development in the area.

PLANNING POLICY

When a planning application for a new house is submitted, the council first looks to see whether the proposal accords with the policies of its Local Plan or Local Development Framework (LDF) – as we saw earlier (see Chapter 4), development plan policies are the starting point for planning decisions. A planning application which conflicts with council planning policies for new houses is likely to be refused, unless you're able to show special circumstances to justify an exception being made. This might

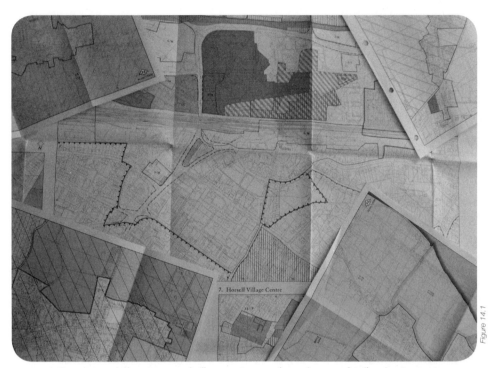

Figure 14.1

Some areas such as town and village centres are shown in more detail on inset maps

appear to be straightforward but, in practice, planning policies are often open to different interpretations.

The most important planning policy distinction is between the locations where the council allows new houses and those where it doesn't. These all-important boundary lines and categorisations of settlements are shown and specified in the policy documents. Your starting point should be to check where your site falls. You can do this by looking at the Local Plan/LDF on-line or at the planning department or by speaking to a planning officer (see Figure 14.1 above). Occasionally, proposals maps aren't clear, for example, where a settlement boundary passes through a plot, it might not be apparent which planning policies should apply; those on one side of the line which are in favour of housing development or those on the other side that are firmly opposed. If so, concentrate your argument on the planning merits of your scheme and try to show that logically it should be considered as part of the village or town, rather than the countryside. Getting planning permission for a scheme which is clearly contrary to council planning policy is extremely difficult, particularly if the site is outside the areas or settlements where houses are normally permitted. In this situation, find out when the LDF is to be reviewed and take advice from a planning consultant on whether there's scope to argue for a change in LDF policies or a change to the areas where they're applied. This is a process that takes years, so you must view it as a long-term possibility.

All levels of planning policy encourage sustainability – minimising use of resources, especially fossil fuels, and pollution – and, in particular, discourage use of private cars. This can affect the location of new homes. Councils see how far new homes would be from facilities, including regular public transport services, shops, employment, education, health care and leisure, and assess opportunities for walking and cycling to such facilities. This sort of information can be included in your supporting letter/statement

or design and access statement. One of the principle means used in an attempt to reduce car use is to restrict parking spaces, although councillors sometimes take a more pragmatic view of this, appreciating that, despite the theory, occupiers will actually want to park cars.

As well as the principle of building new houses, planning policies also deal with design and relationships with other buildings (see Figure 14.2 opposite). Typically, housing policies include phrases such as 'character and appearance of the area', 'high standards of design' and 'residential amenity', which are quoted by planning officers when they don't like your scheme. It's best to avoid arguments about subjective matters and to concentrate on the positive aspects of your proposal and to ask the planning officer to say exactly what aspects of the design he or she finds unacceptable and what changes he or she would like to see. Ultimately, you could ask whether the officer believes the objections on planning grounds are so strong that they justify refusing permission. Some policy and guidance is more technical in nature, dealing with matters like

LOCAL PLAN/LOCAL DEVELOPMENT FRAMEWORK POLICIES FOR NEW HOUSES

Proposals for housing development will be permitted:

Within settlement boundaries provided that the proposal is for the re-use, renovation or re-development of previously developed land or buildings on sites within the settlements. In addition, proposals for the following will be permitted on greenfield sites:

(a) the development of small sites, 0.4 hectare or less within the settlements; or

(b) schemes to provide affordable housing which meet the requirements of policy HS13.

Outside Planning Boundaries planning permission for new residential development will be refused unless:

(a) it is in conformity with the criteria detailed in policy H11 (Rural exceptions policy), or

(b) it is demonstrated by the applicant that there is a clearly established existing functional need for an enterprise to be in a countryside location, there is a proven need for someone to live on site, and that the enterprise is economically viable.

Within defined built-up areas, permission will be given to proposals for residential development where the following criteria are met:

(a) the development does not involve the significant loss of an area of nature conservation or an open or wooded area of land;

(b) the land or building is not within an established business area and is not allocated for any other use in this Local Plan;

(c) efficient use is made of the land in terms of density and as general guidance should be provided at a density of at least 30 dwellings per hectare;

(d) the character and form respects that of the locality

(e) includes a high quality environment for prospective occupiers including appropriate landscaping and open space;

(f) the provision for car parking and vehicle manoeuvring does not significantly reduce garden areas, including front gardens, or adversely affect adjoining property.

Planning permission will be refused for residential infilling outside the Urban Areas or Defined Settlements unless:

1) the site is a small gap in an otherwise built up frontage; and

2) the development does not detract from the rural character of the area or result in the loss of attractive views of the countryside; and

3) the proposal does not consolidate existing development in remote areas or those served by unsatisfactory roads.

The council will favourably consider suitable development on frontage infill and corner sites which are in keeping with the character of the area.

Figure 14.2

energy performance, waste and recyclables storage, internal space standards, minimum garden size, incorporating renewable energy and disabled access. You need to ensure that your designer is aware of the various requirements and, as far as possible, that your building meets the criteria. Where the planning policies insist on detail, you might need to bring in specialists to help in some of these areas, such as calculating energy ratings or advising on the merits and specification of solar power, wind power or ground source heat pumps. If you're not able to comply with technical standards, discuss this with a planning officer and explain and justify this in your application.

Special planning policies apply in Conservation Areas, Green Belts, Areas of Outstanding Natural Beauty, or National Scenic Areas in Scotland, and in areas where development might affect archaeological remains. Planning policy and/or guidance documents state why an area has been given a special designation, so take this into consideration when drawing up your scheme. In a Conservation Area, your design has to respect the local architecture and, in many cases, make use of local materials. In Areas of Outstanding Natural Beauty the appearance of the countryside is paramount, so make sure your siting and design isn't prominent and take advantage of any opportunities there are for landscaping. Councils have their own particular designations and accompanying policies, such as 'Special Landscape Areas' or 'Areas of High Townscape Merit', which you need to take into account – most of these mean that planning applications for new houses will be given particularly close scrutiny.

PLANNING HISTORY

It's important to know the planning history of a site before you make a planning application (see Chapter 4). If your application is for a similar size and design of house to one that has been made on the same site previously, expect the same decision, unless circumstances have changed. Don't concern yourself with the rights and wrongs of earlier decisions but concentrate instead on how your application overcomes problems or is in some way an improvement on previous schemes. For example – that it's for one instead of two houses, it's got a lower roof line or the access has been revised. If circumstances have changed since a previous decision was made, such as other new houses built nearby, a road improvement or a policy change, draw attention to this in your covering letter. The council's file on previous applications, whether approved or refused, provides useful information on the type of house that will be permitted. You can find out the reaction of the highway authority, drainage authority, parish council and neighbours and alert yourself to any possible difficulties with your own application. Look for conditions attached to any previous permission, as this shows you the type of conditions that could be put on your planning permission.

SURROUNDING AREA

How your house would fit into the surrounding area is an important planning consideration, so look at the size of your plot, the size and design of house you want and the position of the house on the site. Compare these with the pattern and styles of houses in the locality. Get ideas for your design by studying the style of other houses in the area, particularly those closest to your site. Look at roof slopes, number of storeys, materials and finishes, distances to boundaries and between buildings and patterns of windows and doors. Study the Ordnance Survey map to get an impression of the pattern of development and make your house consistent with it. In areas of uniform design or with definite character you'll probably have to follow the established style closely but, in mixed areas or an estate of individual houses, you've greater scope. All these factors are considered by the council in the light of its planning policies and design guidelines, although individual planning officers' personal preferences and prejudices could play a part. Examples of what you should consider are shown in Figures 14.3, 14.4 and 14.5 (pages 174-176).

If the planning officer claims that some aspect of your proposed house doesn't fit the established pattern or style of buildings locally, there are a number of ways to overcome his objection. Look first for areas of agreement, then identify the areas of dispute and any where the planning

PATTERNS OF DEVELOPMENT

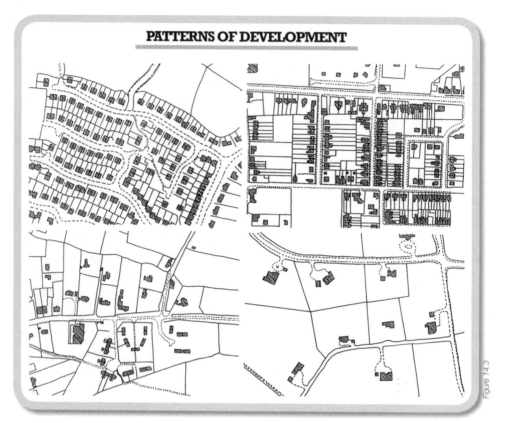

Figure 14.3

Typical patterns of development into which new homes should fit: top left, suburban; top right, town centre; bottom left, village; bottom right, rural

officer might compromise. Slight repositioning of the house or changing external finishes can make a marginal case acceptable. A design that the planning officer says is too prominent could have roof hips introduced, the roof pitch altered and the ground floor level lowered to reduce the height and bulk of the building, without fundamentally altering the amount of accommodation provided. Additional landscaping could help too. When you suspect it's only the planning officer's personal prejudices behind his reaction to your design, ask for specific planning reasons for the objections. So, for example, if you're told brick walls are acceptable but render isn't, ask precisely why and what the

Figure 14.4

New two-storey five bedroom house on well-screened plot giving flexibility over design

difference would be. Objections of this kind are often raised in the hope that your house design will be changed in the way the planning officer wants but without any real prospect of the application being turned down if it isn't.

Where you're not able to negotiate – for example, when the size of the plot is a problem, look for examples of similar houses in the locality. Identify properties of a comparable size or position on an Ordnance Survey map but make sure the map is up to date and check the properties you identify by going and looking at them. It's more effective to give general conclusions from the evidence you collect than a complex analysis so, for example, highlight on a map all the local house plots which are

Figure 14.5

New small infill house attached to the end of a terrace designed for the tight site and different set-backs of adjoining houses

the same size, or smaller, than yours. Your conclusion might be that about half the plots in the immediate area are the same size or smaller than the application site, so it can't be said to be uncharacteristically small or out of keeping with existing properties in the vicinity. Don't bother with a detailed statistical case – planning is an art rather than a science. Try to find examples of other planning permissions in order to overcome objections to the size or design of the house or its siting on the

plot – the best type of evidence is recently built or approved houses. Check the planning files of one or two of the best examples – it's unwise to base your arguments on a property where the planning application was contentious, the committee was divided and the finished product is widely regarded as an eyesore. Precedent is a useful argument, where you can point to a number of applications approved in circumstances identical to your own, but don't rely on this alone.

CHAPTER FOURTEEN ● GENERAL CONSIDERATIONS

The ultimate test for a planning application for a new house in relation to the surrounding area is whether it would cause serious harm. This is difficult to judge, as obviously it's a matter of personal opinion. One person's bold architectural statement is another's hideous monstrosity, and just because a proposed house is different doesn't necessarily mean it's bad, although many councils appear to hold the opposite view. Planning officers' objections to designs are often vague and only justified in terms of the worst excesses of planning jargon, for example 'harmful to visual amenity', 'unneighbourly', 'presenting an uncomfortable juxtaposition with neighbouring dwellings' or 'neo-vernacular pastiche'. You must counter this type of jargon with precise arguments; if a planning officer says your design is unacceptable, consider what the harm would be, who it would affect, where exactly it could be seen from and what would be the effect of landscaping. Get an impression of how your house would look in the context of the surroundings by superimposing a sketch of the house onto a photograph of the plot in its setting. Take photographs of the plot from a number of different angles, enlarge them on a photocopier or computer and sketch in the house but take care to give as accurate an impression as possible, otherwise your drawings lack credibility. If such drawings come out well, they can help to persuade planning officers and impress neighbours and councillors – but only use them if they give a favourable impression. Be objective about the design and layout of your scheme and, if in truth your house doesn't blend into the setting well, it's better to accept this and try to make it compatible than to insist there's no problem.

Where the council won't agree to the type of house you want – because, for example, it says the house is too large – one option is to obtain planning permission and build a house that complies with the council's requirements and then alter it later. Many minor changes, such as adding new doors, windows and extensions, are permitted development and so don't need to be approved by the council (see Part Five) or you can go back with planning applications for more major

Figure 14.6

New three-bedroom replacement bungalow sitting amongst adjoining single-storey houses

changes after a few years when the house is an established part of the local scene. Bungalow roofs can be built to allow for the easy addition of roof lights or dormer windows and room layouts can take account of your plans for future extensions. If you can afford to take a long-term view, and there's little prospect of achieving the desired house at the first application, this is a useful ploy. However, there are potential pitfalls here, as there's no guarantee that you'll be granted planning permission in the future. The council might impose conditions on the planning permission, preventing additions or alterations to the building – often done by removing permitted development rights. Councils also have the power to remove permitted development rights in sensitive areas by making what is called an 'article 4 direction'. These are most common in Conservation Areas but are occasionally found elsewhere. If you plan to build your house and alter it afterwards, do just check with the planning department whether your property is in an area covered by these restrictions.

NEIGHBOURS

The effect a new house would have on neighbouring properties is more tangible and easier to assess than the effect on the wider area, and is the most likely source of opposition to your planning application. The main factors are noise, loss of light and overlooking and, at the planning application stage, the effects must be predicted and

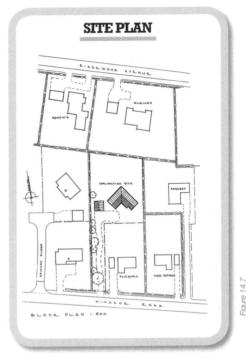

Figure 14.7

Layout to avoid mutual overlooking with windows in surrounding houses and their gardens

Figures 14.8 & 14.9

Examples of overlooked property. Left: house with higher level properties close behind, blocking light and outlook and creating a cramped site layout. Right: bungalow overlooked by two-storey houses behind and lacking garden privacy

taken into account in working up your scheme. Careful siting, design and positioning of windows of a house, together with measures proposed to mitigate effects (such as landscaping), can overcome most potential problems. Examples of what to do and what not to do are given in Figures 14.7, 14.8 and 14.9 on the previous page.

Overlooking windows of habitable rooms in neighbours' houses or their gardens is usually avoided by getting the right layout of rooms and making sure the windows in the proposed house don't look directly into those of neighbours. Overlooking is usually only a problem from first floor windows, because fences provide privacy for ground floor rooms. You can use frosted glass, high level windows and roof lights where windows can't be avoided but, in really severe cases, a bungalow might be the only solution. If you're wedded to a particular house-type or design that would create overlooking, see whether tree planting could overcome the problem. Only evergreen trees create year-round screening but planting rows of quick growing Leylandii conifers

is unpopular with most planning officers – many of whom have an aversion to these trees because of their excessive and often inappropriate use in the past. New tree planting isn't always the answer as it takes many years to establish an effective screen and is unlikely to be accepted by the council as an adequate solution to an acute overlooking problem.

Noise generated by vehicles using an access would be a relevant planning consideration when designing the site layout of a house which we looked at in relation to backland plots (see Chapter 13). Similar effects occur if your site layout involves a garage behind the house or the access passes close to a neighbour's property. Unlike the backland situation, trade vehicles might not have to travel the full length of the drive to reach the house, so overall noise and disturbance is correspondingly lower. If your site has existing houses close by, take particular care over the design of the access to minimise the impact on neighbours.

In areas of high density housing, building a new house can block natural light to an existing house.

This could restrict the siting of the proposed house, the design of the roof, or even the size and shape of the house in order to avoid the problem. If the planning officer or neighbour is concerned about loss of light, look carefully at where sunlight falls in the morning and afternoon and what the difference would be in summer or winter – although the important point is that houses get adequate natural daylight in habitable rooms, which doesn't necessarily mean they have to receive direct sunlight. If you can show that a loss of light wouldn't be severe, it's unlikely to justify refusing your application.

Losing a view or a pleasant vista isn't a planning matter, although often stirs affected neighbours to forceful objection. This could sway a planning officer in a finely balanced case and could certainly influence the planning committee. Look for ways to minimise the effect on neighbours' views by careful positioning of the house on the plot, opting for a low-profile design or lowering the ground level of the proposed house.

When a planning application is made, neighbours are notified by the council, by post or site notice, and often by a notice in the local

paper as well. People don't like change and are understandably anxious about change taking place around their homes, so bear this in mind when drawing up your planning application. Your neighbours-to-be won't be enthusiastic at the prospect of noise and disruption during the building works, even if they've no real objection to a new house. As a matter of courtesy – and in the interests of getting your application approved – discuss your plans with them and try as far as possible to overcome any concerns they have. Approaching neighbours in advance can help establish good relations and prevent objections. You might want to take this a step farther and get their active support by writing a letter in favour of your scheme. Even if your neighbours are happy with your plans and don't object to the application, the council will still look carefully at the effect on adjoining properties and seek alterations if it isn't satisfied. Where a neighbour is likely to object whatever you do, it might be better to avoid telling them about your plans, as an early warning could give them time to organise opposition.

PLANNING APPLICATION
DRAWINGS FOR A NEW HOUSE

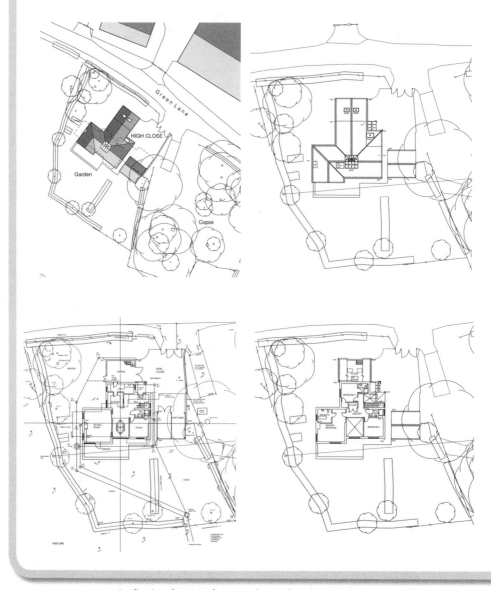

Application drawings for a new home show how the building would fit on the site,

NORTH-EAST ELEVATION

SOUTH-EAST ELEVATION

SOUTH-WEST ELEVATION

NORTH-WEST ELEVATION

Figure 14.10

all sides of the house and its floor and roof plans (courtesy of Constructive Individuals)

183

newbuilds

4

CHAPTER 15

SPECIAL CASES

The site and general considerations apply whenever a planning application is made for a new house, whether it's a small urban infill plot or a large suburban or rural site. There are, however, a few situations where slightly different considerations apply – namely where an existing house is being replaced, where the new house is occupied in connection with agriculture and mobile homes.

REPLACEMENT DWELLINGS

Replacing an existing house is one of the few ways in which you can get planning permission for a new house in the countryside. Where you want to demolish and replace an existing house there are two initial points to consider: first, whether the residential use of the building has been abandoned; and second, what size of replacement house will be permitted. These questions are especially pertinent in places where planning policies generally restrict new houses being built.

Abandonment is often an issue where a disused or derelict house is replaced in the countryside because, where the original use has been given up, a new planning permission is needed to re-establish the principle that a house could be built on the site. In a rural situation this is normally very difficult. There's no hard and fast rule defining abandonment but generally a house is deemed to have been abandoned if its residential use ceased deliberately, it's derelict, there's been another use or it's been vacant for a long period of time. You'll, therefore, need to research the history of a property that's been empty for some years, before you make an application to replace it. You might find out all you need to know from local people or, if not, try the old rating records kept by the council which show when domestic rates were paid on the property. Fortunately a residential use isn't easily abandoned and even one ceasing 30 years ago has been held by the courts not to have been abandoned. Dereliction doesn't in itself amount to evidence of abandonment but you can't expect to build a replacement

house where all that remains of the original building is one wall and some foundations (although, in one exceptional appeal decision, an aspiring self-builder managed to do just that). If you're in doubt about whether abandonment has occurred, take professional advice or ask a planning officer how the question of abandonment is normally interpreted by that council – but do this carefully. Avoid saying the building is derelict, as this gives the wrong impression so describe the house simply as 'empty' to avoid any implication of abandonment.

Local planning policies vary in their treatment of replacement dwellings in the countryside – some give criteria restricting the new dwelling to a specific percentage larger than the existing one, others are more general and permissive, whilst some only allow replacement in exceptional circumstances. Where you want to replace an existing house, look carefully at the Local Plan or Local Development Framework (LDF), or speak to the planning officer regarding local policies (see Figure 15.1 overleaf). Generally, it's important to minimise the bulk and impact of a new house

LOCAL PLAN/LOCAL DEVELOPMENT FRAMEWORK PLANNING POLICIES FOR REPLACEMENTS

Planning permission will be granted for the replacement or rebuilding of an existing dwelling outside the urban areas and defined settlements provided:

i) the proposed dwelling is of a size and scale similar to the original dwelling; and

ii) the dwelling being replaced is, or was recently, permanently occupied as a dwelling unit, was originally constructed of materials appropriate for a permanent dwelling and contains at least one living area plus a separate room for toilet and washing facilities; and

iii) the proposed replacement or rebuild is acceptable in its setting by virtue of its scale, design, siting and materials and would not adversely affect the character or nature conservation value of the area; and

iv) the original dwelling is demolished upon completion of the replacement dwelling at the latest.

Outside defined built-up areas proposals to replace existing single dwellings will be permitted on a one for one basis if:

(A) the residential use has not been abandoned;

(B) highway, access and parking requirements can be met;

(C) the new dwelling is appropriate to its setting and is not obtrusive in the landscape, particularly in an area of outstanding natural beauty; and

(D) the new dwelling does not change significantly the scale of the existing building and is appropriate to its built and natural setting.

Figure 15.1

on the rural surroundings but this doesn't necessarily mean the new house must be small. For example, the replacement of a full two-storey house by a chalet bungalow with a much larger floor area might be acceptable because the chalet would be less prominent. The replacement of a pair of semi-detached cottages with a single larger house, again might be justified on the basis of reduced traffic movements and general activity associated with one, as opposed to two. The use of local designs and materials usually makes a new house more acceptable to the council and might enable them to overlook policy restrictions and accept a larger replacement.

AGRICULTURAL DWELLINGS

Exceptions are occasionally made to the general restriction on building new houses in the countryside where there's a genuine need for accommodation for a farmer or agricultural worker. Agriculture means any type of farming, horticulture or forestry. Equestrian uses, such as stud farms, riding schools or liveries, aren't, strictly speaking, agriculture but can sometimes justify

planning permission for a house in the countryside. Similarly, other uses for which a rural location is essential can sometimes justify a dwelling. Councils give close scrutiny to planning applications for agricultural dwellings, especially where new or small agricultural enterprises are involved, so don't imagine you can buy a few acres of agricultural land together with some chickens, call it a farm, and get permission for a house. Unless the council is convinced the business is genuine, it won't grant planning permission for a new house and will, in any event, often give planning permission for a mobile home for a temporary period of a few years, to enable the business to become established and prove the need for a permanent house. Councils expect to see evidence of:

■ experience or qualifications in agriculture;
■ significant investment in the business;
■ a financially viable business, or a business plan working towards viability;
■ the need to live on the farm rather than in the nearest town or village.

Thorough preparation is the key

to a successful application. You should submit detailed information to support the need for a house on the property and prove the viability of the business. Proving need is crucial – the need must result from the activity of the farm and not the financial or personal circumstances of the applicant. For example, cows calving or pigs farrowing have to be tended day and night and horticultural enterprises using sophisticated propagation equipment need 24 hour monitoring. Get support from the appropriate farmers union and a report from an agricultural consultant to verify technical points and give your case greater weight. Need also arises from security considerations, so if thefts or vandalism occur on a farm, report this to the police, keep a record and use it as evidence. Councils check the validity of applications by consulting agricultural advisers and you can often contact them direct to discuss your proposal. Proving financial viability involves providing your business accounts for recent years or drawing up a detailed business plan showing how viability is going to be achieved. Viability means the land and

business must generate sufficient income to support you, this is usually not less than the current minimum wage.

Where the council decides to accept the need for an agricultural dwelling, normal planning considerations apply to its siting, appearance and access arrangements. The scale of house permitted is usually the minimum necessary to serve the needs of the farm. This often means a bungalow or modest three bedroom house, although it's occasionally possible to get permission for a larger house. Planning permission for an agricultural dwelling is normally granted subject to conditions restricting its occupation to someone engaged in, or retired from, agriculture and their dependants. Councils sometimes prevent the house being sold off from the farm through a planning obligation/agreement (see Chapter 1), tying the house to the farm. Planning permission for agricultural dwellings is a complex matter, so take professional advice at an early stage.

MOBILE HOMES

Mobile homes are sometimes

Figure 15.2

Sub-standard 1960s timber bungalow suitable for replacement

used by people building houses as temporary accommodation while they build their new home. However, having planning permission for a new home doesn't mean that you have permission for a mobile home on the plot. Unless you're going to be fully employed in the construction of the house, strictly speaking, you're supposed to get planning permission for a mobile home. Not everyone fits this definition, although 'fully employed' does include being employed in the management rather than the physical construction of the house. Making a planning application takes time and costs money and in most cases it's unlikely to be refused, as you're only asking for temporary permission. Evicting you from your own plot takes the council considerable time and expense and your house would probably be finished and the mobile home gone before the action against you was concluded. If you do make a planning application, site the mobile home in an unobtrusive spot, well out of the way of the building works.

If you want to live in a mobile home for a longer period of time, or permanently, you need planning permission and a site licence. Permission is unlikely to be given in established residential areas as a mobile home would be out of character there and in the countryside, mobile homes are governed by the same restrictive planning policies as new houses. Despite this, you can see examples of mobile homes in suburban, rural and holiday areas – some of these don't have planning permission but are long-established and so the council can't take enforcement action to remove them. Others are in gardens of homes, where planning permission isn't required as long as the mobile home is used as additional space for the main house. You're meant to apply for permission, however, if the mobile home is used for self-contained accommodation or is outside the garden, such as in an adjoining paddock.

Mobile homes and caravans are often stationed on leisure plots for holiday use. Such plots are frequently agricultural land that's been sub-divided. In these cases, although planning permission might not be needed for temporary siting of a mobile home, it's needed for the change of use from agriculture to leisure. Ensure there's planning permission – check this with the council before buying such a plot or stationing a mobile home on one. None of this applies to permanent, licensed mobile home parks which have planning permission for a number of homes on the site. Provided that number isn't exceeded, no further permission is needed to station your mobile home there.

CHAPTER FIFTEEN ● SPECIAL CASES

PART 5:

PLANNING PERMISSION FOR OTHER PURPOSES

P lanning permission is needed for many types of project and work beyond building new houses from scratch – obtaining the necessary permission for these can be equally difficult. There are particular factors to take into account with each type of project and ways of presenting applications that give them the best chance of success. You should know about and consider these points before you make a planning application. This section tells you which types of domestic development need permission and how best to obtain it.

5

CHAPTER 16

HOME CONVERSIONS

Many existing buildings are suitable for conversion – barns, oast houses, churches, pubs, warehouses, even railway stations and public loos – and these often make interesting homes of unique character. Using the fabric of an existing building can save money when creating a new home but where substantial work is required, such as under-pinning foundations or stripping and recladding walls, a conversion can cost at least as much as a new building. Conversions sometimes provide an opportunity to live in places where planning permission for new houses wouldn't be granted, such as in the countryside or in a Conservation Area, because conversion is often allowed as a means of preserving buildings that are architecturally or historically valuable.

The conversion of buildings for residential use needs planning permission, as a change of use will be taking place and almost inevitably the exterior of the building will be altered in some

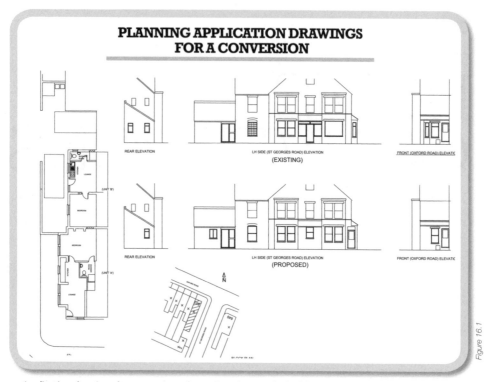

PLANNING APPLICATION DRAWINGS FOR A CONVERSION

Application drawings for conversions show alterations to the building and how the space will be used (courtesy of Woolhampton Design Centre)

way – for example, the installation of new or different window and door openings. Converting outbuildings in the grounds of a house into self-contained living accommodation needs planning permission, if the building is to be occupied separately from the main house (if it isn't to be separately occupied, see Chapter 20). Planning applications for conversions are made in full, rather than outline. In most cases, you need to include floor plans and elevations of the building as it is and with its proposed changes but check with the planning officer to see what drawings the council requires (see Figure 16.1 above). Occasionally, an existing building is so dilapidated or incapable of conversion that it would have to be completely demolished and either rebuilt as it was before or replaced. The planning considerations in those cases are

LOCAL PLAN/LOCAL DEVELOPMENT FRAMEWORK
PLANNING POLICIES FOR CONVERSIONS

Planning permission will not be granted for the conversion of rural buildings for residential purposes unless the following criteria are met:

(A) the building is capable of conversion without extension or substantial alteration and makes a valuable contribution to the rural surroundings, and

(B) the applicant has evidence of attempts over a period of at least 12 months to put the building to commercial use, tourism and community uses, and

(C) the building is sited in a location appropriate to its surroundings.

A change of use to housing will be considered provided:

A) the building does not fall within a defined employment area; or

B) it does not involve the loss of protected open space; or

C) it is not in a primary or secondary shopping frontage as shown on the proposals map (unless it is above ground floor level); or

D) the building can provide satisfactory living conditions.

Proposals for the re-use or adaptation of existing buildings in the countryside will be permitted provided:

(A) the form, bulk and general design of the existing buildings are in keeping with their surroundings; and

(B) the existing buildings are suitable for the proposed new use(s) without needing extensive alterations, rebuilding and/or enlargement; and

(C) the conversion would not have a detrimental effect on the fabric, character and setting of historic buildings; and

(D) the conversion respects local building styles and materials; and

(E) the proposed curtilage of the new development is not visually intrusive or harmful to the amenities of the surrounding countryside; and

(F) the proposed new use(s) would not generate traffic of a type or amount harmful to local rural roads, or require improvements which would detrimentally affect the character of such roads or the area generally; and

(G) the proposed new use(s) would not result in material harm to the environmental qualities of the surrounding rural area; and

(H) the use of the building by protected species is surveyed and mitigation measures are approved by the council using expert advice.

The council will encourage proposals which bring upper floors above shop units and surplus office accommodation, outside preferred and established industrial locations, into residential use.

Figure 16.2

the same as for new houses and you should follow the advice in Part Four.

When you find a building that has potential, the first point to check is the council's policies on conversions (see Figure 16.2 on page 195) which are set out in the Local Plan or Local Development Framework, or sometimes in separate supplementary guidance booklets. These documents usually give the criteria which the council applies to applications and can be a useful guide to assessing your prospects for a successful conversion. Alternatively, phone the planning department and ask about the council's views on conversions. The policies set out the types of building and the locations where the council believes conversion is appropriate. Planning policies often distinguish between those buildings in settlements and those in the countryside and, as with new houses, policies in the countryside are likely to be more restrictive. Conversions in settlements are normally allowed, especially in existing residential areas and, where the existing use of a building has undesirable effects on neighbours, such as

noise or high levels of traffic. In some places, however, particular uses are protected, for example, local shops in residential areas, pubs in villages or traditional craft industries, and policies here might be against conversions that would mean losing those uses.

Where a building lies outside the council's defined settlement boundaries, planning policies often only allow conversion if the building has architectural merit (either individually or as part of a group) and can no longer be used for its original function. Even here, councils' first choices are for changes of use to commercial purposes to provide local employment or holiday letting to bring in tourists' money, rather than to residential use. Planning policy often requires potential conversion buildings to be marketed for 6-12 months for business purposes to ascertain whether there's a demand for such use, before granting permission for residential use. Evidence of the marketing effort has then to be submitted with the application. Conversions to houses can also be discouraged by planning policies where buildings are in open countryside, such as

Figure 16.3

Rural building suitable for conversion to a small dwelling

an agricultural building prominent in the landscape, because of the activity the use would introduce, as well as fences, garden buildings and drives.

The building must be physically capable of conversion, which means you must look at such points as the internal layout, ceiling heights and structural stability. At an early stage, you should get a survey drawing of the building showing the existing layout and heights of rooms, door openings, window positions and stairs, which you can use to work out your proposed layout and design. You might want to introduce new floors or take out walls and so must establish that the structure will be able to withstand this. You also need to take account of building regulations requirements, as these can influence design. Planning isn't concerned with structural matters but with the changes that would be made to the building and whether it could actually be converted, rather than rebuilt. Sometimes councils ask for a structural survey to be carried out and a report submitted with a planning application, to prove that the building is capable of being converted. Take advice from a building surveyor on structural matters and building regulations requirements.

Where the existing building has some architectural value, proposals for conversion can be difficult. The most valuable buildings are Listed, to give them additional protection, and Listed Building consent has then to be obtained from the council as well as planning permission. Listing covers not only the structure of the building but also its interior and any attached structures. Conversion proposals for Listed Buildings are looked at very carefully and you're expected to preserve the important architectural features of the building. You can find out if a building is Listed by looking at the council's records or by asking a receptionist at the planning department. On one hand, conversion can give an important building a viable use and so save it from deterioration but on the other, residential conversion can change the very character of the building

that's supposed to be preserved. In these cases, councils might refuse planning permission in the hope that some other use will be proposed that doesn't affect the building to the same extent.

Conversion schemes for architecturally valuable buildings, whether Listed or not, have to be sensitively designed, so it's worth getting your application drawings prepared by a building designer with experience of working on historic buildings. External changes are expected to be kept to a minimum and those that are necessary must be consistent with the style of building – so, for example, fitting new dormer windows and adding chimneys wouldn't usually be allowed in barn conversions, as they're not traditional features of a barn. Internal design should respect the layout of the original building, including height and space, which sometimes means that you must have open-plan living areas. Similarly, adding extensions and porches, building garages and outbuildings and even laying out gardens can all have an impact on the building and its setting and the council takes these factors into account in assessing your application. Building materials used in conversions should

Figure 16.4

Garage/store converted to a one-bedroom dwelling

match the existing materials which might mean you have to use local stone, second hand clay peg tiles, stock bricks or oak timbers.

District councils have specialist officers or advisers who deal with building conservation and architectural matters and it's worth speaking to them, as the planning officer will consult them when you make your planning application. Arrange an initial meeting with the officer at the property and talk to him about your plans, note what's said and comply with the suggestions as far as you can. The officer might also be able to give you the names of building designers and builders who specialise in your type of project. When you have draft application drawings, send a copy for the specialist's comment but try to distinguish between the officer's personal design preferences and genuine planning objections.

One issue that can come up with conversion applications is the question of the original, or last, use

Figure 16.5

Church converted into a substantial open-plan house

of the building and whether it's likely to continue or resume. Where the building has been empty or up for sale for some time this is less likely to be an issue but, if not, you may need to explain why the building can't continue in its existing use. Evidence of unsuccessful marketing by an estate agent might be required to prove there's no longer any demand for previous use. Speak to the planning officer about this and include information to back up your claim in a covering letter when you submit your application. Where

the building still has a use that has undesirable effects on neighbours or the area, describe this in your letter and, if possible, ask the affected neighbours to write in support of your application.

Where you want to convert an old barn, or similar rural building, bear in mind it could be the habitat of protected bats or owls. The council might insist on a wildlife survey before validating your application. Speak to the council to find out whether a survey would be required and consider getting one carried out

Figure 16.6

Converted garages and storage sheds (courtesy of Barry Page)

early on to make sure this wouldn't be a problem.

In making your assessment of whether you'll get planning permission and in working up a design, think about the surrounding area and neighbouring properties. A residential conversion in a commercial or industrial area or on a working farm, might not be appropriate because of the conflict between uses. Conversions are expected to comply with most standards that apply to new houses, such as providing safe access, parking spaces, private garden areas and suitable drainage. Greater latitude is often given, though, as achievement of the standards isn't always possible because of physical constraints and this is especially true where the building has architectural value. In planning internal and external layout and where to put new windows, consider the possible effect on nearby houses – the council will be concerned about protecting the privacy an enjoyment of neighbours.

5

CHAPTER 17

HOME EXTENSIONS

Extending your home is an alternative to, and can be a better option than, moving house – you might be very attached to your existing house, its setting, location and neighbourhood – and moving house is expensive and disruptive. The price of houses with more bedrooms, a second bathroom or additional reception rooms could be out of your reach, an extension can give your family the extra space it needs and, at the same time, add significantly to the market value of your home. However, if you think about extending only as an investment, do your sums very carefully and obtain valuations from estate agents and estimates of building costs from a builder or a building surveyor first.

There are permitted development rights which allow you to build extensions, within specified limits, without needing to make a planning application (see Figure 17.1 opposite). It's always worth checking with a planning officer that what you propose is permitted development before starting any

PERMITTED DEVELOPMENT RIGHTS
FOR EXTENSIONS (ENGLAND)

Extensions to dwellings can be built subject to the following main limitations:

Maximum 50% site coverage, excluding the area of the original dwelling;

Not higher than the existing building;

Not in front or to the side of a wall facing a road or public right of way;

Single-storey can't project to the rear of the original dwelling more than 4 m for detached dwellings and 3 m for other houses, or be higher than 4 m;

Two or more storeys can't project to the rear of the original dwelling more than 3 m or come closer than 7 m to the rear boundary and the roof pitch has to match the original dwelling;

Side extensions can't be higher than 4 m or one storey and can't be wider than half the original dwelling;

Maximum eaves height 3 m within 2 m of any boundary;

Conservation areas/AONBs – no extension beyond original side walls and single-storey only at the rear;

Materials have to match appearance of existing dwelling, apart from conservatories;

Side windows above ground floor to be obscure glazed and only opening at high level.

Notes   Original house for this purpose means the house as built or as it was in 1948.

No rights for flats or maisonettes.

Permitted development rights can be restricted by article 4 directions,

conditions or legal agreements.

Figure 17.1

work, though. Planning applications for extensions can be controversial, because in many instances they're built very close to other houses and can affect the owners' enjoyment of their properties. Personal circumstances are more likely to be taken into account by councils when assessing extension applications but they don't override significant planning objections. Whether or not you have to make a planning application, ask the planning department if the council has published design guidance for extensions, as this can give you useful pointers. Where a planning application is required, the council will

LOCAL PLAN/LOCAL DEVELOPMENT FRAMEWORK PLANNING POLICIES FOR EXTENSIONS

Planning permission will only be granted for the extension of permanent dwelling houses in the rural area provided that proposals would not:

1) by itself, or together with the existing building, create a dwelling which is readily capable of conversion into more than one dwelling;

2) detract from the rural character and appearance of the existing dwelling and/or of the surrounding area, by virtue of scale, mass or design, particularly the Areas of Outstanding Natural Beauty where proposals should not detrimentally increase the bulk of the building visible from public vantage points;

3) detract from the established amenities of adjoining residents.

When determining applications for extensions and alterations to existing houses and bungalows within the built-up areas, account will be taken of the need to maintain a range of types of housing in each locality and proposals will be required to meet the following criteria:

(A) the design, size and scale of the extension is in keeping with the existing dwelling AND surrounding dwellings, and does not have an adverse impact on the character of the locality;

(B) the proposal does not result in an overbearing or unneighbourly form of development detrimental to the amenities of nearby residents;

(C) the character and style of the existing property is retained or improved; and

(D) the proposal includes sufficient car parking spaces within the curtilage of the dwelling and conforms to highway and access requirements.

In considering development proposals, account will be taken of the need to maintain a range of types of housing in each settlement.

Extensions and alterations to dwellings will normally be permitted providing:

i) the scale, design, materials and site coverage would be satisfactory in relation to both the existing property and any predominant characteristics of adjoining properties or the area as a whole;

ii) the proposal would not adversely affect the appearance of the street-scene by occupying space between buildings which should remain open;

iii) the proposal would not result in an unacceptable degree of overlooking or overshadowing of neighbouring property or have an overbearing effect.

Proposals which are not in accordance with the detailed advice given in the Council's Residential Design Guidance, will not normally be permitted.

Figure 17.2

urge you to comply with its guidance even though, in some cases, this goes beyond what it can properly insist on. Some Local Plans and Local Development Frameworks (LDFs) set out general criteria for extensions (see Figure 17.2 opposite), which are usually more restrictive in countryside areas. Here councils generally try to limit all new building and restrict the size of extensions by, for example, imposing a floor area limit based on a given percentage of the original house. A good building designer can usually come up with ingenious designs to maximise space and get around the rigid application of councils' limitations.

The main issues with extensions are the effect on the appearance of the house itself, the effect on the surrounding area and the effect on neighbours. Design is largely a matter of personal taste, although councils often try to get applicants to conform to their views, for example, avoiding flat roof extensions. They can only insist on points like this where there would be serious harm to the outward appearance of the structure. It's desirable for extensions to compliment the original house in terms of proportions, building

materials, roof slopes, window types and positions (see Figures 17.3 and 17.6 on pages 206 and 211). If you employ a building designer, he or she should be familiar with these points and can also show you how to achieve an efficient layout which makes the most of the space. Front and side extensions are most likely to affect appearance and so should blend with the main building which, when extended, shouldn't then clash with other houses nearby. This is more important where properties in the street have a uniform appearance and less so in areas with a mix of styles. The concept of a building line is often mentioned, although it has no formal status and is only significant where there's a clearly established line which is an important characteristic of the area. Side extensions can alter the appearance of a street, especially on estates where houses have uniform gaps between them. This effect is known as 'terracing' as the semi-detached or detached properties appear to become a terrace when all the gaps are filled by extensions.

Extensions of Listed Buildings and houses in Conservation Areas need to be carried out with particular care, so think about getting help from a suitably experienced building

Figure 17.3

Side extension matching the materials and design of the main house yet set back and with a lower ridge to leave the original house clearly defined

designer. Work on a Listed Building must have Listed Building consent and demolition in Conservation Areas must have Conservation Area consent, in addition to planning permission. There are reduced permitted development rights in Conservation Areas. The design of an extension must respect the style and architecture of the house and leave its important features intact. Where you want a relatively large amount of extra accommodation

in a house, the special character of which would be lost if extended, one solution can be to build a separate building, perhaps joined to the main house by a single-storey link.

Often, even more controversial than appearance, is the effect of an extension on neighbours. This is the most common reason why planning applications for extensions are turned down. The issues here are: the effect on privacy, both indoors and in gardens through

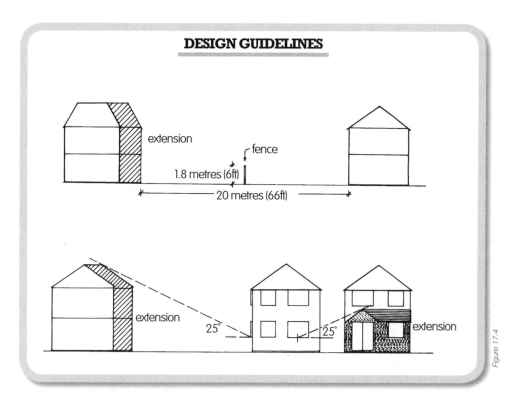

DESIGN GUIDELINES

extension

fence

1.8 metres (6ft)

20 metres (66ft)

extension

25°

25°

extension

Figure 17.4

Some councils publish design guidelines for extensions including distances between buildings

overlooking; loss of daylight in rooms of adjoining houses; and extensions being overbearing. Single-storey rear extensions with windows facing into the garden don't generally cause loss of privacy problems but two-storey extensions with side windows or roof terraces often result in overlooking. This can usually be overcome by thoughtful design – look at adjoining houses and see where their windows are, particularly sitting rooms,

dining rooms, kitchen-diners and bedrooms (habitable rooms). Try to come up with a design that avoids windows directly facing these or rear gardens close to the back of adjoining houses. Oblique views don't generally cause a problem but, if facing windows are unavoidable, use obscured glass and non-opening main window casements. Councils' design guidance sometimes states the minimum distance necessary between facing windows at the rear of houses (see Figure 17.4 overleaf). If your proposed extension comes within that distance, check the actual circumstances to see whether there would be overlooking and consider moving your windows.

When looking at the possible loss of daylight in rooms in adjoining houses, differentiate between habitable and non-habitable rooms, the latter being bathrooms, utility rooms, halls and landings, etc. Extensions shouldn't block all daylight reaching windows of habitable rooms but this factor carries less weight where a room has windows in more than one aspect. Daylight in this sense doesn't necessarily mean direct sunlight. Householders have the right to put up a 2 metre (6 foot 8 inch) fence along their boundary and various other permitted development rights to build not only extensions, but garages and outbuildings, all of which could block daylight. The council should take these rights into account in assessing your proposal. There's a rule of thumb guide, known as the 45 degree rule, for the design of extensions to prevent the loss of daylight. Variations of this rule are included in many councils' guidelines (see Figure 17.4 overleaf).

Two-storey extensions close to boundaries can be overbearing for neighbours, although this is largely a subjective factor to weigh up in each case and would have to be significant to justify the refusal of planning permission. Clever designs, such as hipped roofs and lowering eaves levels, can sometimes reduce the apparent bulk of buildings, without affecting floor area. Councils often ask for a minimum distance to be left between extensions and boundaries, typically 1 metre (3 feet 3 inches). Whilst this is sensible to allow you access for maintenance and cleaning, councils shouldn't insist on it in the absence of sound objections on grounds of appearance or affect on boundary hedges or trees. Similarly, some councils have guidelines for the amount of garden area that a house should have but the loss of garden shouldn't generally be used as an objection to an extension.

The issue of setting a precedent should rarely be relevant to planning applications but it can apply to extensions in some situations, such as terraces and estate houses. You could find planning permission is refused, not because your proposal is unacceptable in itself, but because it would establish an undesirable

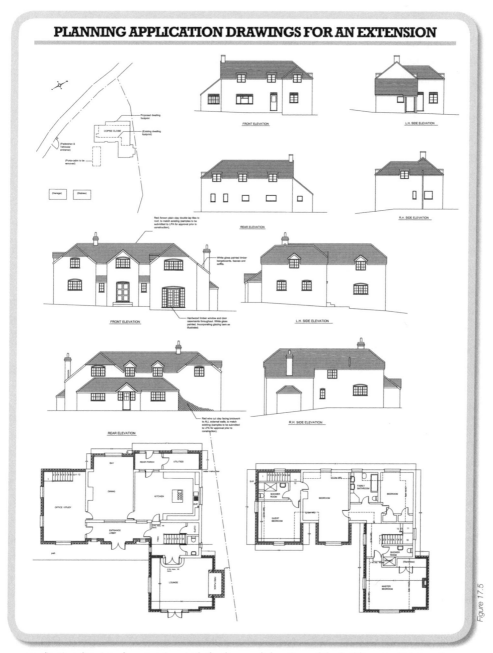

PLANNING APPLICATION DRAWINGS FOR AN EXTENSION

Application drawings for extensions include plans and elevations of the building as existing and as proposed (courtesy of Woolhampton Design Centre)

Figure 17.5

precedent which could be followed by your neighbours. Similarly, just because other extensions have been allowed locally doesn't mean that yours will be allowed – there could be cumulative impact which would affect the appearance of the area and policies and guidance change over time. Unfair as this might seem, such decisions have been confirmed at appeal.

Planning permission for an annexe can cause problems. The considerations are essentially the same whether it's a new building, conversion or mixture of both. If a building or part of a building is occupied completely separately from the main house, planning permission is needed and it's assessed as a new house. If the annexe is occupied as part of the main house, permission is only needed for the new building work and is, therefore, much easier to obtain. The dividing line between the two situations can be very fine, particularly where the occupants are relatives or staff working in the main house but the interpretation can often be crucial to planning permission. Councils tend to look for points like separate access, internal connections, what facilities the annexe would have and the relationship between

occupiers. The more self-contained the annexe, the closer the council will look at how it will be occupied. Where you want an annexe or converted outbuilding to be used as part of the main house, and the officers seem concerned, you can help reassure them by including an internal connection or shared parking areas or, in extreme cases, by avoiding separate entrances or full kitchens in your application drawings. An alternative is for the council to attach conditions or ask for a legal agreement to prevent a separate living-unit being created. On the application form, describe the proposal as an extension and don't go into details about how you plan to occupy it, unless you're specifically asked to by the planning officer. If you're converting an outbuilding, check first that the building work needs planning permission, as it might well not, and don't describe it as a conversion but as alterations.

Planning applications for extensions are usually straightforward. Remember you don't have to go into great detail in your description on the application form. The drawings are the most important part and these should include floor plans and elevations of the building, both as it is and after

Figure 17.6

Chalet-style side extension providing extra accommodation in a way that is subordinate to the main, full two-storey house

extension (see Figure 17.5 on page 209). If the extension is very small, drawings just showing the building after extension might be sufficient but check first with a planning officer or administration officer who validates applications. If appropriate, explain in a covering letter why you need more space – a growing family, an elderly relative moving in with you or some special needs – as compelling personal circumstances might influence the decision. Where your extension would provide your house with basic facilities which it lacks or are sub-standard, mention this in your letter, especially when the proposal doesn't comply with the council's guidelines. If you're on good terms with your neighbours, speak to them about your plans and, if they're concerned, do your best to meet their objections. It's far better to resolve potential problems this way rather than when the application is submitted. Neighbours often feel happier with a proposal if they've been consulted and you've taken the time to discuss it with them first.

5 *alterations*

CHAPTER 18

HOME IMPROVEMENTS

This chapter concerns the main types of improvement and alteration work you're likely to carry out on your own house – loft conversions, porches, replacement windows, cladding and rendering, re-roofing, painting and balconies. Some of these are covered by automatic rights under the permitted development rules, which allow you to carry out the work without having to apply for planning permission (see Figure 18.1 opposite). Permitted development rights are more restricted in Conservation Areas, National Parks, Norfolk and Suffolk Broads and Areas of Outstanding Natural Beauty, and councils can take away other rights in defined areas, often Conservation Areas, or by conditions on planning permissions. The rules aren't always easy to interpret and you might not be aware of restrictions on your property, so it's always worth checking with a planning officer before you start. Most alterations to Listed Buildings need separate Listed Building consent,

PERMITTED DEVELOPMENT RIGHTS FOR HOME IMPROVEMENTS (ENGLAND)

Dormer windows and roof extensions

Not higher than the highest part of the existing roof

Not in the front roof slope where it faces a road or public right of way

Terrace houses – maximum 40 cubic metres larger than original roof

Other houses – maximum 50 cubic metres larger than original roof

Can't include a veranda, balcony or decking

No rights in conservation areas/AONBs

Materials have to match appearance of existing dwelling, apart from conservatories

Must be set back 20 cm from eaves, apart from hip-to-gable extensions

Side windows to be obscure glazed and only opening at high level

Roof lights

Must not project more than 150 mm

Re-roofing

No restrictions where no additional volume created

Solar panels

Must not project more than 200 mm or be higher than the highest part of the roof

Conservation areas – not on the front or sides where they can be seen from a road or public right of way

Porches

Maximum 3 sq m measured externally

Maximum 3 m high

Not within 2 m of a boundary with a road or public right of way

Replacement windows

No limitations

Cladding

No rights in Conservation Area, AONBs, National Park or the Broads

Painting

No adverts, directions or announcements

Notes: *No rights for flats or maisonettes*

Permitted development rights can be restricted by article 4 directions, conditions or legal agreements

Figure 18.1

regardless of whether you have to make a planning application.

LOFT CONVERSIONS

Using loft space for living accommodation doesn't in itself need planning permission but the external work, such as dormer windows, does. Under permitted development rules (see Figure 18.1 on the previous page), dormers are generally allowed at the rear and sides of roofs, but not in the principal elevation (which in most cases is the front of the house) where it faces a public road or path. The type of box dormers at the front of houses, which were common, are no longer allowed without a planning application. All dormers in Conservation Areas and the other specially protected areas require a planning application to the council.

Planning applications have to be accompanied by drawings showing the house from each side, with the proposed dormers. Finding the right design can take some skill if, for example, your house has a hipped roof. Since creating rooms in the roof also needs building regulations approval and usually involves cutting roof timbers, it's worth having a good set of drawings prepared by

an experienced building designer. Many councils have design guidance for dormers, which you can obtain from the council's website or planning department. This is probably helpful, even where you don't actually need the council's permission. Guidance usually includes:

■ not breaking ridge lines;
■ keeping dormers small and not dominant;
■ using the same roof pitch as the main roof;
■ setting dormers below the ridge and back from the face of the building;
■ using two small dormers instead of one long one;
■ tile hanging to match the roof;
■ avoiding box dormers in most cases.

Where a planning application is required, the council will assess your proposal to check how visible the dormer would be from public places and whether it's in keeping with the house, adjoining buildings and the street. Dormers are often prominent because they're at such a high level and can't be screened.

The shape of roofs can be a unifying factor on the appearance of estates and can have a greater visual impact in terraces and dormers. Similarly, the symmetry of semi-detached houses can be lost. Where houses in the area aren't identical or where others already have dormers, planning permission is generally easier to obtain. The council also checks for potential overlooking, so take account of the position of neighbours' windows. New windows at the front and back don't usually cause problems, but side windows sometimes can. Roof lights, which fit more or less flush with the roof slope, are outside the definition of development requiring permission or come within permitted development rules, including where they would face a public road. The use of roof lights can sometimes overcome possible objections to dormers but, although overlooking is less likely, it can still be used as an argument against roof lights by planning officers.

PORCHES

Porches are usually straight-forward but, if they exceed the permitted development criteria (see Figure 18.1 on page 213), you must make a planning application. The council would look at the effect on the appearance of the building and would expect to see materials which match or compliment the house.

Figure 18.2

Pitched roof dormer window requiring an application because it faces a road

REPLACEMENT WINDOWS AND ALTERATIONS

Like-for-like replacement windows and minor alterations don't need planning permission, although permission has been required in cases such as putting up false shutters, replacing wooden sash windows with aluminium and uPVC and replacing one large window with two smaller ones. You're also allowed to replace or alter windows under the permitted development rules, including installing double glazing, providing the materials appear similar to those in the existing house and unless the council has specifically taken those rights away. The latter is unlikely to have been done except in a Conservation Area or some other particularly sensitive area. So, if your house is in a Conservation Area, check the need for planning permission with the council before going ahead with the work. Remember, alterations to a Listed Building are likely to need Listed Building consent and flats don't have permitted development rights.

In sensitive locations, councils are likely to want replacement windows and alterations to maintain the existing or original style of the house and area. This might mean replacing like-for-like – double hung timber sashes or leaded lights rather than using factory made units in modern materials. The fact that some of the neighbouring properties have had architecturally inappropriate double glazing installed isn't likely to help you, as this might be the very reason why the council took away the permitted development rights in your area.

In cases where you have to make a planning application, ask the planning officer what drawings you need to submit, as a full set of drawings might not be necessary.

CLADDING AND RENDERING

In Conservation Areas, National Parks, Norfolk and Suffolk Broads and Areas of Outstanding Natural Beauty, or where the council has specifically taken away permitted development rights, you need to apply for planning permission to clad the outside of your house. In all other areas it's more difficult to tell whether a planning application is required, as changes to the permitted development regulations (in England) have confused the issue. Your best bet would be to get confirmation from your council as interpretations might vary. Where a permission is needed, the council looks at the appearance of the building and surrounding properties. In areas of uniform design or with particular features, such as distinctive local brickwork, a completely different external finish probably wouldn't be allowed.

RE-ROOFING

Re-covering a roof with identical or similar materials doesn't need planning permission at all. Re-roofing with different materials comes within the permitted development rules, as long as the shape of the roof stays the same. Again, the council can take away this permitted development right but is only likely to do so in a Conservation Area or other sensitive area where it would want to see original materials used.

EXAMPLES OF PERMITTED DEVELOPMENT

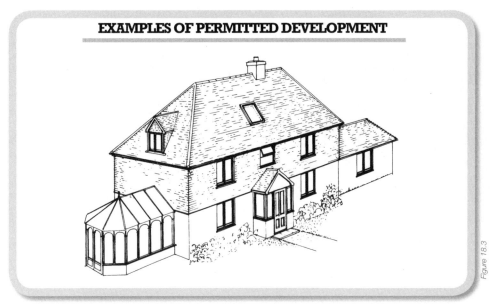

Figure 18.3

Permitted development rights for home improvements include: conservatory; dormer window; roof light; tile hanging; porch; replacement windows and extension

PAINTING

Repainting a house the same colour doesn't need planning permission and painting it or repainting it a different colour is permitted development. This means that in a limited number of especially sensitive areas – for example, Georgian and Victorian squares where buildings are a uniform design and colour, the council can remove rights to paint and repaint and control this work by requiring a planning application to be made. Listed Building consent can also be needed if you want to paint a Listed Building a different colour.

BALCONIES

The use of the flat roof of an existing building as a balcony doesn't require planning permission, although railings, parapet walls and forming door openings for access from the house to the roof might require an application. There are no permitted development rights that allow the creation of a new balcony. This sort of project is best checked with the council, especially where neighbours might be concerned about overlooking.

5

CHAPTER 19

SUB-DIVIDING HOMES

Large houses are often suitable for division into two or more separate houses or flats. They can be too big for modern family needs or the character of the area might have changed creating a demand for smaller units. Sub-division can include dividing a large country house into two houses, converting a suburban villa into ground and first floor flats or converting a four-storey town house into a number of units. Such conversions can be a way of preserving old buildings and grants are sometimes available for the work. Sub-dividing a house or flat into two separate units always needs planning permission but, as with annexes, the question of what constitutes a separate unit isn't always straightforward (see Chapter 17). The test is how the building is occupied – whether there are separate cooking and eating facilities, electricity and gas metres, entrances and washing facilities and whether there's internal access between the parts. The main issues upon which planning applications for sub-division are generally assessed are related to the effect that the proposed use would have on the area, the effect any external alterations would have on the building and providing satisfactory living conditions. Councils' planning policies that can affect sub-division applications typically cover:

■ retaining family accommodation in certain areas;

■ encouraging the provision of small units;

■ minimum size of house suitable for conversion;

■ minimum unit or room sizes;

■ parking provision;

■ amounts of garden space.

It's debatable how rigidly councils should apply such policies, as some of these factors relate to personal choice of the occupants but this doesn't help you much if the council is inflexible, as your only redress might be to go through an appeal. Look up relevant planning policies in the Local Plan or Local Development Framework (LDF), or speak to a planning officer about your proposal and ask how other similar applications have been decided. The increase in cars and parking used to be a common reason for sub-division being refused planning permission. In town centres, sites close to public transport and where the units are

Figure 19.1

Substantial house in a town too large for modern needs makes a suitable sub-division into flats

small and likely to be occupied by people without cars, parking provision is often less crucial. Objections can include:

■ more traffic movements in and out of the property;

■ insufficient off-street parking;

■ increased on-street parking affecting the appearance of the street and highway safety;

■ the appearance of the building being affected by parking provided in front of it;

■ parking spaces at the rear of the property affecting neighbours and reducing the amount of garden.

Councils sometimes object to sub-division on the grounds that the character of the area would suffer. If you're faced with this, ask the planning officer for specific points to back up the objection. The reasons could be the change in the appearance of the property or street, additional noise and activity or the intensive use of the property being at odds with all others in an area. Councils sometimes claim the types of occupier and their presumed behaviour would harm an area but this is speculation and very difficult to substantiate.

When working up a planning application, start by getting a measured survey of the existing building, showing room layouts, doors, windows, stairs and where drains run, and the site. You have to make a full planning application and so must submit drawings showing the proposed layout and any external alterations (see Figure 19.2 opposite). Unless the sub-division is clear and obvious, use a building designer to draw up the scheme, as he or she will be familiar with achieving workable layouts, maximising the use of available space and also complying with Building Regulation requirements.

Decide whether a vertical or horizontal division would work best – in most cases, it's desirable for each unit to be self-contained with separate services, facilities and entrances, if possible. Think how the separate units relate to each other – for example, keeping bathrooms close together or above one another so they can use the same ducts and drains. Where possible, avoid rooms, such as bedrooms and living rooms, next to or above each other although the sound insulation standards in the building regulations are now so stringent that this is less of an issue. In some instances you'll need to divide up the garden and grounds and, where family accommodation is created, most councils would expect this to have its own private garden space. Providing separate garden and parking areas can add to the attractiveness of the scheme but where you're creating a number of flats, a communal garden is usually sufficient. Find out what parking requirement the council has and meet it if you possibly can. Where you can't, discuss this with a planning officer at an early stage as it could be fundamental to whether permission is granted. Show defined parking spaces on your site layout plan and look for as many opportunities as possible for screening cars and access drives, which should also be shown on the drawing.

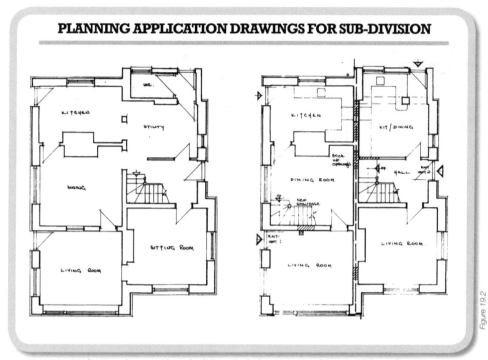

PLANNING APPLICATION DRAWINGS FOR SUB-DIVISION

Figure 19.2

Application drawings for sub-division include existing and proposed floor plans

Your planning application must include floor plans and site plans of the building as it is and as proposed. If the conversion involves external work, such as new doors, windows, dormers or extensions, you need to show those changes on elevation drawings. Where you can't meet particular guidelines in the council's guidance on sub-division, explain why not in your covering letter and point to any mitigating factors. Look around the area for similar schemes that have been successfully carried out and that aren't causing any problems, and refer to them in your letter.

If the property is Listed you'll probably need Listed Building consent, so the design has to be worked out with special care. Listing includes the interior of the building and there might be features that have to be preserved. External alterations, such as new drain pipes and changes to windows, could harm the appearance of the building. However, if sub-division is accepted in principle, a skilled designer should be able to come up with solutions.

5

CHAPTER 20

BUILDING IN YOUR GARDEN

There are permitted development rights, subject to various size and location restrictions, which allow you to build most of the usual types of garden buildings – like garages, sheds, greenhouses, swimming pools – as well as laying hardstandings and building tennis courts (see Figure 20.1 opposite). There are sometimes opportunities to extend your garden and trees in your garden might be protected by Tree Preservation Orders. In this chapter we look at what you can and can't do in your garden without permission and what factors influence a decision on planning permission, if you need to apply for it.

GARAGES

In many gardens it's possible to build a garage that comes within the permitted development rules and so you don't have to make a planning application but double-check with the council first. Common situations where permission is needed are when

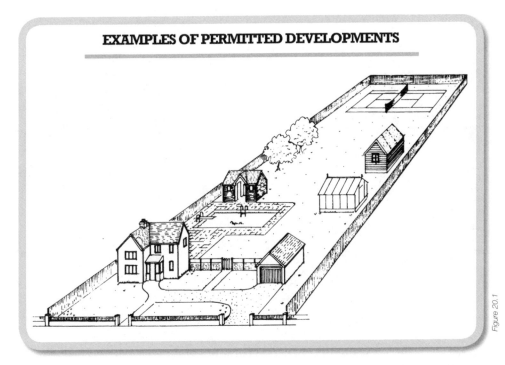

EXAMPLES OF PERMITTED DEVELOPMENTS

Figure 20.1

Permitted development rights for building in gardens include: access drive; garage; fences; paving; swimming pool; pool house; greenhouse; shed and tennis court

a garage has to be positioned in front of the house or, in Conservation Areas and Areas of Outstanding Natural Beauty (AONBs), at the side of the house. Where you have to make an application, the council has control over its location and design. Some councils' planning departments publish design guidance for garages which usually encourages pitched roofs and materials that match the house and discourages prefabricated types

of construction. The council assesses planning applications for garages on their appearance, the effect on neighbours and the amount of garden land or vehicle turning area that would be taken up.

Look around the area at existing garages. If there's already a range of styles, you'll have more freedom in your choice of design and the council is less likely to insist on its guidance being met. Other structures that have

Garage requiring an application as it is in front of the house, over 4 m high and two-storey

Figure 20.2

been built nearby are particularly important if you want to put your garage in front of your house or an established building line in estate and urban situations. Garages here can be prominent but in other cases trees, hedges and fences reduce prominence and make such a location more acceptable. Building a garage at the front of your house can be justified on sloping sites where the alternative would be a steep drive up to a garage at a high level above the street. Car ports are affected by the same considerations as garages but are often not so popular with planning officers because of the use of cladding materials such as corrugated plastic. There should be space within the site to stop a car in front of the garage clear of the pavement or road, leaving room for the garage door to open. In tight situations, a car port might overcome this problem. In deciding where to position your garage, take account of the effect on neighbouring houses.

The council looks at factors such as blocking daylight and whether the building appears overbearing, just as it would for extensions (see Chapter 17). If you want windows in your garage or possibly to include a workshop with a window, avoid placing this where it would overlook a neighbour's windows or garden. Where your application shows a large workshop area, the council might add a condition to the planning permission preventing any business use taking place.

Permitted development rules allow you to lay hardstandings for parking and to open an access on to an unclassified road (ie most minor and estate roads). Hardstandings in front of the house over 5 sq metres either have to be made of porous material, or surface water has to drain to a permeable area in the garden. If the road is classified A, B or C, you have to make a planning application for a new access. The council looks at the effect of losing a wall, hedge or trees, particularly in a Conservation Area, where cars would be parked on the site, the benefits of providing off-street parking and highway safety.

Councils usually expect there to be space to turn cars around on site so they don't have to reverse out into the road. If you would have to park in front of the house, look for opportunities to provide screening and check how many other houses nearby have a similar arrangement.

GARDEN BUILDINGS

The permitted development rules include most garden buildings, subject to size and location limits (see Figure 20.3 on page 227). Such buildings must be for the normal enjoyment of the house, rather than, for example, for a business or other purpose. Planning applications are usually needed only when these buildings would be in front of the house or more than one storey, when they would take the amount of building in the garden over the 50 per cent limit or, in the case of a fence enclosing a tennis court, it would be over 3 metres (10 feet) high. Rounded plastic covers over pools are subject to the 3 metre (10 foot) rule and so a planning application should be made for one any higher than this. There are much reduced rights in Areas of Outstanding Natural Beauty and none in the grounds of Listed Buildings.

Garden buildings can only be built under permitted development rules within the grounds of your house (or 'curtilage', as the regulations calls it). In most cases, this is clear cut and the curtilage is the garden around your house inside your boundary fences but in others it can be more difficult – where, for example, there's an attached paddock or a large area of land. The fact you own the land or whether it's divided by fences, doesn't decide the issue – it's the area cultivated and maintained as a garden that's important. Speak to a planning officer or get advice if you have any doubts. If you can prove a building outside the curtilage has been in place for four years, the council can't make you take it down (although, perversely, might be able to stop its use).

Garden buildings allowed as permitted development include those built to house poultry, bees, pet animals, birds or other livestock for the 'domestic needs or personal enjoyment' of the occupiers of the house. These buildings could be stables, aviaries, kennels, pigeon lofts or chicken coops. This is sometimes a controversial area. Where, for example, animals are bred or trained, there could be an element of business, or stray animals are looked after, the purposes might not necessarily relate solely to the enjoyment of a house. What's generally considered reasonable often depends on the numbers of animals involved – councils can take action to reduce the number of animals kept at a house. The point about buildings only being permitted development if they're in the curtilage often comes up in connection with horses. Stables and sand schools aren't supposed to be built in paddocks and fields which lie outside the curtilage, without making a planning application.

Where you have to make a planning application for a garden building the issues are likely to be positioning, effect on neighbours and, in sensitive locations only, design and materials. You still need to submit application drawings, so it's worth asking the supplier of the building for these or councils sometimes accept drawings or photographs from brochures.

PERMITTED DEVELOPMENT RIGHTS FOR BUILDING IN YOUR GARDEN (ENGLAND)

Outbuildings, enclosures and swimming pools

Maximum 50% site coverage, excluding the area of the original dwelling

Not in front of the dwelling

Single storey only

Maximum heights – 4 m for pitched roof buildings; 2.5 m for buildings within 2 m of a boundary; and 3 m in other cases

Maximum eaves height 2.5 m

Not in garden of a Listed Building

Conservation Areas, Areas of Outstanding Natural Bueaty, National Parks and Broads – more than 20 m from the dwelling buildings maximum ground coverage 10 sq m

Conservation Areas – not at the side of the dwelling

Fences, walls and gates

Maximum height 1 m adjoining a road used by vehicles or 2 m in other cases

No rights for Listed Buildings

Hard surfacing

Front gardens – over 5 sq m of surfacing must be porous or drain to a permeable area in the garden

Access to an unclassified road

Must be required in connection with some other category of permitted development

Notes: *No rights for garden buildings or hard surfacing for flats or maisonettes*

   Permitted development rights can be restricted by article 4 directions, conditions or legal agreements

Figure 20.3

GARDEN IMPROVEMENTS

Most types of work you might carry out in your garden, such as laying paths and patios and putting up fences, are permitted development (see Figure 20.3 above). Rights to put up fences, walls and gates at the front of houses on some open plan 1960s and 1970s housing estates were taken away by conditions on the original planning permissions to maintain the appearance of the estates. There are no automatic rights to put fences or walls around a Listed Building and so you have to apply for planning permission. To qualify as permitted development, strictly speaking the fence has to enclose an object or area, so a free standing decorative fence or wall isn't covered but a retaining wall can be. Except along boundaries with a road, fences can be up to 2 metres (6 feet 8 inches) high, but any higher than this and an application to the council is needed. The council might be concerned about the effect on neighbours, in terms of its appearance and blocking windows and daylight.

If any trees in your garden are covered by a Tree Preservation Order, you must get the council's consent before working on or felling the trees. If you live in a Conservation Area, you have to give the council notice that you intend to carry out work on any tree (see Chapter 13). Speak to the district council's tree or landscape officer in the planning department for information about this.

Where your house is next to agricultural or other open land, the possibility of extending your garden by taking in some of the adjoining land can come up. Unless the land is already part of a garden, planning permission is required to change the use to residential. This is a fact many people aren't aware of and they sometimes suffer the consequences when the council takes action to stop it being used as garden. Councils can't take action after ten years of the date the change of use took place. If the land concerned is agricultural and you intend using it for grazing horses, planning permission isn't normally needed but it would be for any stables or other buildings erected on it. Getting permission to extend your garden can be difficult where there's a clear division between existing gardens and countryside and where the land is designated Green Belt, National Park, Area of Outstanding Natural Beauty/ National Scenic Area or other local policy designation. Councils are often concerned about the change in appearance from fields to cultivated gardens with associated sheds, greenhouses

and washing lines. Councils
can put conditions on planning
permissions taking away
permitted development rights
to help prevent this happening.
You can sometimes justify the
proposal with arguments that
your existing garden is very
small or you need extra land, for
example, to provide an access or
to serve a septic tank.

5

CHAPTER 21
BUSINESS USES

ore people now are working from home and many small businesses start life in a spare room in a house or shed in the garden. There's a wide range of businesses that might operate from, or in a home: office and professional; medical consultancy; craft and light industry; catering and providing bed and breakfast. You don't always need planning permission for part business use but where you do there are common issues which arise. We'll look at these factors in this chapter.

The first question to consider is whether you need planning permission for your use at all. Up to a certain point, part business use at a house is ancillary to the normal residential use and so doesn't need permission. The test is whether the business use is noticeable and so can be distinguished from a purely residential use. This depends on factors such as the number of visitors coming and going, traffic levels, types of vehicles,

Figure 21.1

Medical treatment rooms attached to a house requiring permission because of the scale

noise levels and fumes or smells. Where these go beyond what the house might normally be expected to generate, planning permission is needed. Uses such as child minding are unlikely to need permission because looking after a few children is a normal residential activity. Similarly, providing bed and breakfast in one or two rooms or having a lodger doesn't normally need permission. Parking a commercial vehicle on a public road is beyond the council's scope of planning control but there are cases of councils stopping commercial vehicles being parked at houses as this isn't considered to be associated with normal residential use. It's worth bearing in mind that inspectors who decide planning appeals work from home. These examples of actual cases illustrate when permission is required.

NO PLANNING PERMISSION NEEDED:

■ garden shed used as an office for the home and business;

PLANNING APPLICATION DRAWINGS
FOR PART BUSINESS USE

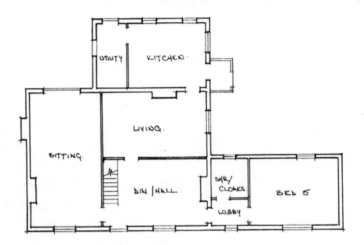

GROUND FLOOR - EXISTING

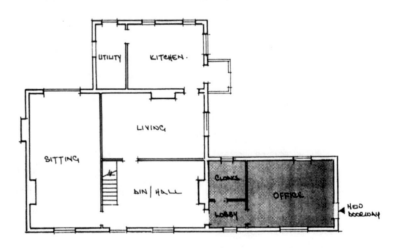

GROUND FLOOR - PROPOSED.

Application drawings for part business use include existing and proposed floor plans

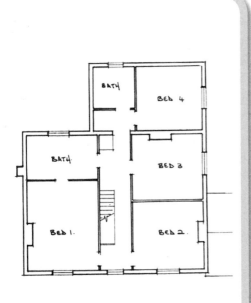

FIRST FLOOR - EXISTING

FIRST FLOOR - PROPOSED

Figure 21.2

■ study in a ten room house used as an office where there were no callers;

■ surgery treating three patients a week.

PLANNING PERMISSION NEEDED:

■ plumbing business using a shed for storage, the house for administration and parking three vehicles;

■ two rooms in a house equipped as offices for two/three people;

■ garage used to administer 20 employees generating up to ten vehicle journeys a day.

The level of activity for which you should get planning permission isn't clear cut and it's often best to just continue, so long as your business activities aren't harming anyone. The council is only likely to take action to stop or restrict your business use if neighbours complain. However, if starting or continuing a business use means spending significant amounts of money on your property or if you plan to buy a house specifically because it offers scope to live in and also run your business, get the planning position established first. Speak to a planning officer about what you propose or take professional advice from a planning consultant and, if there's any doubt, apply for planning permission to put the matter beyond question. Just because a business use is significant enough to need planning permission doesn't, of course, mean it's so harmful that it would be refused. In assessing an application, the council looks at the effect on neighbours, parking, road safety and any changes in appearance. Think whether there'll be any effect on neighbours through noise or activity, try to contain the business use inside buildings and put in sound insulation, if appropriate. Where your business has run successfully for some time and your neighbours are completely happy about it, ask them to write in support of your planning application when it's submitted. The neighbours will be consulted in any event, so it's worth getting them on your side.

Keep a note or estimate the number of visitors and vehicle journeys which the business generates. In areas without good public transport but with limited on-street parking, show if you can that there's sufficient space for staff and visitor parking on-site without taking up all the manoeuvring room. Keep cars and activity as far away from adjoining properties as possible and look for opportunities to provide screening by planting or fencing. Where the business generates a significant level of vehicle movements, make sure the access is a suitable standard or could be improved, for example, so that cars can pass each other and there's good visibility (see Chapter 7). Try to confine the storage of materials inside buildings or, failing that, at the rear and keep them as well screened as possible. Pipes, timber, components or equipment strewn around the site or visible from public places won't impress a planning officer.

Your house or outbuildings might need some conversion work to make them suitable for your business use, for example new windows or doors. If so, bear in mind considerations such as overlooking your neighbours and consistency with the architecture of the house. Where you need a new building or extension to expand or locate your business, the factors to take into account are the same as for other buildings and extensions (see Chapters 17 and 20). Remember, permitted development rights for building and alterations at your house relate only to work arising from the needs of normal residential uses.

Check with a planning officer first but your planning application for part business use normally needs to be accompanied by a block plan and/or floor plans (see Figure 21.2 on pages 232-233) and, if new building work or alterations are involved, elevation drawings as well (see Chapter 7). Usually it's appropriate to define the application site (by drawing a red line on the location plan) as only the parts of the house or outbuildings used by the business. If there are some areas or rooms that you want to use for business and home purposes, include those in the red line but describe the proposal as a mixed residential and business use. The council might want a parking area allocated within the application site so ask the planning officer about this. Where you intend to provide additional parking, landscaping, fencing or sound proofing or to improve an access, show these clearly on the application drawings. You need to complete an additional form when making planning applications for commercial

purposes, which asks basic information about the business. In a covering letter describe all the positive aspects of the business and processes involved, trying to make it sound as low-key as possible. If equipment and machinery is used, describe in simple terms what it does, how often it's used and whether it makes any noise. Where you have existing premises elsewhere, you could invite the planning officer and/or councillors to visit to see and reassure themselves the use isn't harmful.

Councils often put conditions on business use at home, limiting the hours of all or some operations, making sure that the business accommodation is only used by occupants of the house or making the permission personal to you. Planning permission is sometimes granted for a temporary period, either to assess its effects or to give you time to relocate somewhere else. This is really up to the council to decide but you can make suggestions as to what restrictions you'd be prepared to accept. This might help your chances of getting planning permission.

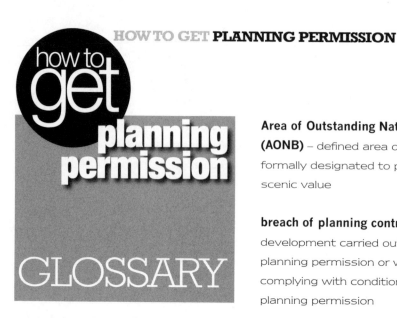

how to get planning permission

GLOSSARY

agent – any representative who acts for an applicant for planning permission or appellant

AONB – see Area of Outstanding Natural Beauty

appeal questionnaire – standard form completed by a council giving details of an appeal that is sent to the Planning Inspectorate and appellant

appeal statement – written case in support of, or opposing, an appeal that is considered by a planning inspector

appellant – an applicant for planning permission who appeals against the council's decision

applicant – individual or body that applies for planning permission

Area of Outstanding Natural Beauty (AONB) – defined area of countryside formally designated to protect its scenic value

breach of planning control – development carried out without planning permission or without complying with conditions on a planning permission

CLG – Communities and Local Government, central government department which deals with planning in England

commissioner – see Planning Appeals Commission

conditions – restrictions or limitations attached to a planning permission sometimes requiring further approvals

decision letter – letter sent to appellant, council and others by a planning inspector giving the result of an appeal and reasons for the decision

decision notice – document setting out the result of a planning application sent to an applicant by the council

delegated decision – determination of a planning application taken by

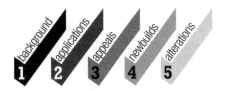

a planning officer on behalf of the council

deferred decision – decision of a planning committee to put off determining a planning application pending further information or action

Design and access statements – evaluation of design, layout and access arrangements submitted with certain planning applications

developer – individual or body that carries out development but usually used to describe those who develop for profit rather than for their own use or occupation

Development Control Advice Notes (DCANs) – statements of government planning policy for Northern Ireland each covering a particular topic

development control officer – planning officer dealing with planning applications and appeals rather than planning policy

development plan – formal title for Local Development Framework, Structure and Local Plan, or the Unitary Development Plan

Directorate for Planning and Environmental Appeals – body that administers the work of reporters who decide planning appeals in Scotland

district council – local government responsible for a district within a county dealing with most day-to-day planning matters including planning applications (used in this book to include city and borough councils and unitary authorities)

enforcement – collective term for council's powers to deal with unauthorised development

enforcement officer (also known as planning investigation officer) – council officer responsible for investigating unauthorised development and complaints about development made by the public

full planning permission – consent to carry out development that includes all details of buildings, layout, access and alterations

Green Belt – land around certain major towns and cities formally designated to stop urban sprawl and protect countryside

hearing – procedure for deciding planning appeals where an inspector leads a discussion about the main issues between the appellant and council

inspector – see Planning Inspectorate

Householder appeal service – simplified method of written appeals for domestic development in England

landscape officer (sometimes known as tree officer) – council officer responsible for trees, tree planting schemes and landscape matters

Lawful Development Certificate (LDC) – document issued by a council stating that planning permission is not needed for the development specified in the application

Listed Buildings – buildings and structures recorded in a statutory list given additional protection because of their special historic or architectural value

Local Development Framework (LDF) – collective name for written documents and maps setting out council planning policy and guidance (England)

Local Development Plan (LDP) – collective name for written documents and maps setting out council planning policy and guidance (Scotland and Wales)

Local Plan – single document comprising maps and a written statement setting out a council's policies for new development and controlling development in its area, being replaced by Local Development Frameworks in England and by Local Development Plans in Scotland

local planning authority – council with responsibility for planning matters

local review process – method for reviewing delegated planning application decisions in Scotland instead of appealing

material considerations – factors which should be taken into account in making planning decisions, such as government advice, special designations and the nature of the site and its surrounding area

National Park – specially protected area of attractive countryside, with its own authority dealing with planning, designated to preserve and enhance its natural beauty and

to promote its enjoyment by the public

National Planning Policy Guidelines (NPPGs) – statements of government planning policy for Scotland each covering a particular topic

National Scenic Area – area of attractive countryside in Scotland formally designated to protect its scenic value

neighbour notification – letter sent to people near a site letting them know that a planning application has been made

outline planning permission – consent to carry out development in principle with some or all of the details left to be established later, cannot be given for changes of use including conversions

parish council – local government body covering a parish within a district, made up of elected councillors who have no legal powers to decide planning applications but often have influence with the district council (used in this book to include town and community councils)

permitted development – types of development given planning permission automatically by a central government order which removes the need to apply for a planning permission

Planning Advice Note – statement of government planning policy for Scotland covering a particular topic

planning agreement – see planning obligation

planning appeal – challenge to a planning application decision or failure to make a decision decided by a central government appointed inspector, reporter or commissioner

Planning Appeals Commission – body which administers the work of commissioners who decide planning appeals in Northern Ireland

planning application – application made to a council for permission to carry out building work and changes of use of buildings and land

planning consultant – professional who advises clients on development proposals and planning law, procedure and practice

Planning Inspectorate – body that administers the work of planning inspectors who decide planning appeals in England and Wales

planning obligation – legal document signed by a landowner, usually in connection with a planning application, requiring him to contribute towards the cost of infrastructure, to carry out specified work or to limit the use of land and buildings

planning officer – local government employee who carries out the work and implements the policies of the council, gives technical advice to council committees and information to members of the public

planning permission in principle – consent to carry out development in outline in Scotland, with some or all of the details left to be established later, cannot be given for changes of use including conversions

Planning Policy Guidance Notes (PPGs) – statements of government planning policy for England each covering a particular topic, being replaced by Planning Policy Statements (PPSs)

Planning Policy Policy Statements

(PPSs) – statements of government planning policy for England and for Northern Ireland each covering a particular topic

proposals map – plan showing the area covered by a Local Development Framework or Local Plan indicating where various policies apply and identifying sites allocated for development

public inquiry – formal hearing open to the public where cases for and against a development proposal are made and examined by an inspector, reporter or commissioner

reporter – see Directorate for Planning and Environmental Appeals

reserved matters application – application made to a council for the approval of details of layout, scale, appearance, access and landscaping after outline planning permission has been given

Scheduled Ancient Monument – archaeological remains or structure included in a statutory schedule, given additional protection because of its national importance

Scottish Planning Policy (SPP) –

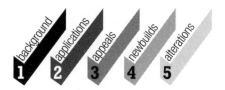

statements of government planning policy for Scotland each covering a particular topic

section 106 agreement – see planning obligation

site notice – formal notice put up on a property to publicise a planning application or public inquiry

Site of Special Scientific Interest (SSSI) – area formally designated to protect its particular wildlife or geological features
SSSI – see Site of Special Scientific Interest

Strategic Development Plans (SDPs) – planing policy document setting out the broad development strategy and planning policies for a council or group of councils in Scotland

Structure Plan – written document with a key diagram setting out the council's broad development strategy and planning policies for a county or group of local councils, now being replaced

Technical Advice Notes (TAN) – statements of government planning policy for Wales covering a particular topic

TPO – see Tree Preservation Order

Tree Preservation Order (TPO) – document identifying single trees, groups, areas or woodlands that are protected from any work or felling without permission

Unitary Development Plan – planning policy document in areas with single-tier councils fulfilling the functions of a Structure and Local Plan, being replaced by Local Development Frameworks (England) and Local Development Plans (Wales)

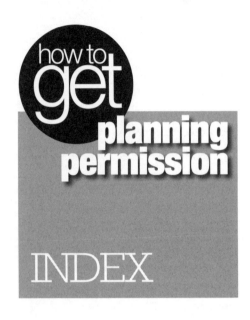

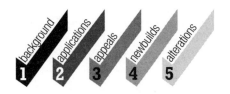

More great property books

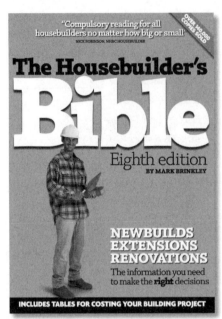

The Housebuilder's Bible is unique - the first book in its field to mix information and advice with detailed yardstick costings for residential building projects. This edition has been completely redesigned with new tables and improved illustrations - all in colour for the first time. Experienced construction professionals have expressed amazement at the amount of detailed information in the book. It works for newbuilds and extensions alike.

How to Find and Buy a Building Plot is the first and only comprehensive book specifically about buying land on which to build a house. It gives you all the essential information you need to locate, assess and purchase a plot. With more than 65 illustrations, tables and examples it is written in a clear and accessible style and is of as much benefit to professionals as it is to the thousands of families who begin land-searching each year. Written by Roy Speer & Mike Dade this is a fully revised third edition of the book.

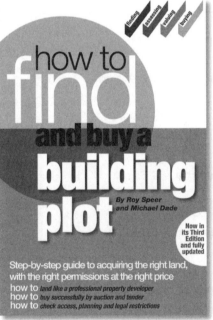

Available from all good bookshops, online, or by phone 24 hours on 01480 893833

from the same publisher

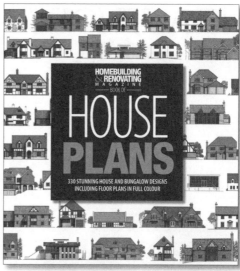
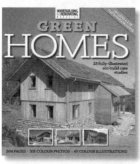

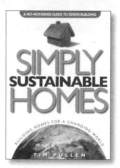

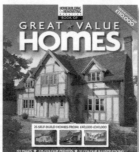

THE AUTHORS

Michael Dade and Roy Speer are consultants, writers and speakers on planning and land matters. Both are Chartered Planning and Development Surveyors with degrees in Estate Management. They run their own specialist town and country planning practice, Speer Dade Planning Consultants, carrying out a wide range of work throughout the country for their book readers, individuals, builders/developers, landowners, businesses and other organisations. Their consultancy work includes making and advising on planning applications, appeals and enforcement, giving evidence at hearings and public inquiries, carrying out planning potential reports, and a useful, cost-effective advice-by-post service for readers.

Roy Speer and Michael Dade can be contacted on:
01273 843737 or 01825 890870
roy@speerdade.co.uk
mike@speerdade.co.uk

GETPLANNINGPERMISSION.CO.UK